Celestial Navigation

for Yachtsmen

Revised Edition

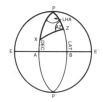

by Mary Blewitt

Edited by Thomas C.

International Marine
Camden, Maine

Published by International Marine®. First published by Adlard Coles Ltd., a subsidiary of A&C Black (Publishers) Limited, London.

10 9 8 7 6 5

Library of Congress Cataloging-in-Publication Data
Blewitt, Mary
    Celestial navigation for yachtsmen / by Mary Blewitt —Rev.ed.
    / ed. by Thomas C. Bergel
    p.   cm.
    "Based on the 10th British edition (1990)"—Editor's note.
    Includes index.
    ISBN 0-07-005928-4 (alk. paper)
    1. Navigation   2. Nautical astronomy   3. Yachts and yachting.
I. Title.
VK555.B667 1994
527—dc20   94-3087
                                                  CIP

Questions regarding the content of this book should be addressed to:
International Marine
P.O. Box 220
Camden, ME 04843

Questions regarding the ordering of this book should be addressed to:
The McGraw-Hill Companies
Customer Service Department
P.O. Box 547
Blacklick, OH 43004
Retail customers: 1-800-822-8158
Bookstores: 1-800-722-4726

♻ *Celestial Navigation for Yachtsmen* is printed on recycled paper containing a minimun of 50% total recycled paper with 10% postconsumer de-inked fiber.

Printed by R.R. Donnelley & Sons, Crawfordsville, IN
Design and Production by Dan Kirchoff

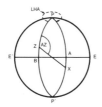

Contents

The Theory

The Practice

Notes

Appendices

Forewords

I am glad to be able to contribute a short foreword to this book because, having studied the text, I am sure that it will satisfy the very real need for an up-to-date work based on the use of the simplified tables and written entirely from the yachtsman's, as opposed to the airman's or ship navigator's, point of view.

Rigorous exclusion of unnecessary material from the text has, in my view, added to the value of the book and made it easier to attain that most desirable thing—correct emphasis on the various aspects of the subject. The result is lucid and practical, but there is just sufficient theoretical explanation included to inculcate the knowledge that is necessary as a basis for this subject.

By the late Captain (E) J. H. Illingworth, R.N.

When Mary Blewitt wrote her admirably concise guide to the principles and practice of astro-navigation at sea, shortly after the war, methods of sight reduction had already become greatly simplified by the introduction of direct-entry (Alt./Az) tables and the GHA almanac. She was at that time a successful navigator in ocean races, in such famous craft as *Bloodhound* and *Myth of Malham*; and her severely practical aim was to provide the yachtsman with sufficient information to make the best possible use of his sextant, timepiece and tables. The book has stood the test of time and, through successive revisions and changes in navigational practice, continues to give sound advice on the whole matter of sights at sea. It has now in effect become a standard work.

The author, as Mary Pera, was later to become Secretary of the Royal Ocean Racing Club and, in due course, Chairman of the Racing Rules Committee of the Royal Yachting Association. Her contributions to navigation have been many, but none has perhaps been more abiding than this seamanlike little volume.

By M. W. Richey,
Director of the Royal Institute of Navigation

Preface

Long ago, in 1938, my father and I were struggling with the intricacies of cosines and haversines, of Right Ascension, Mean Sun and other horrors, when a little book called *Dreisonstok* fell into our hands. One of the earliest of the modern tabular systems, it enabled us to work out our sights in a tenth of the time. Then during World War II we learned the simplicities of the tables designed to assist the airmen in their desperate search for easy and accurate position finding. Later, the more conservative navies followed suit and the scene was set for the sailing navigator to benefit. This was the first navigational revolution in this century: the one exploited by the first (UK) edition of this book in 1950. Since then, a second, more profound, electronic revolution has taken place. In the past, sailing offshore without "astro" was a dangerous hit-or-miss performance, a return to the times of Columbus. Today, yachts race across the oceans using GPS and other navigational aids with no sextant on board. And this is fine, provided of course—and it is a very important proviso—that the instruments function correctly and that the batteries stay in a condition to operate the electronic equipment. Ocean voyaging is obviously safer with the new instruments, but just as a driver needs contingency plans for a flat tyre, so a navigator needs a fall-back when sophisticated instruments fail. Offshore, that fall-back must be astro.

I have written for beginners—or for those who have forgotten all they knew—and I have presumed them to be as ignorant and confused as I was when I began. In the interests of simplicity, therefore, some statements are slightly inaccurate, and there is no mention of such technicalities as the celestial equator or the celestial horizon. You need only add and subtract. As in all navigation, the most difficult part is judging the accuracy of the information obtained, and assessing the weight that can be put on it. If you do not know whether your position line (however obtained) is one mile out or twenty, it is as if you had never taken the sight. Your real work will begin after you have absorbed this book and begin to observe often enough to form your own opinion of the value of your sights.

Few amateurs can hope to reach the standard of a professional navigator—or should I say old-time professional navigator?

Regular daily observations over the years gave them confidence and accuracy; but nevertheless you will be able to take adequately competent sights, even in rough seas, and I can assure you that a sense of triumph when a sight proves correct is well worth the effort involved. It is the first step that is difficult; take one sight and you will be bewildered, take two and light dawns, take a dozen and you will wonder what all the fuss was about. I hope that the explanations in this book are clear enough to encourage you to go and take a sight with a good idea of what you are trying to do and a modicum of confidence that you will be able to do it.

My warm thanks go to Thomas Bergel for his skillful revision of the text that brings the book right up to date.

Mary Blewitt
Colchester, Essex, England
April 1994

Editor's Note

This Revised Edition of Mary Blewitt's now-classic book is based on the 10th British Edition (1990). The principal changes I have made are:

1. Addition of running fix from two Sun sights.

2. Addition of a discussion and comparison of the several so-called "short" tables, based on the method of H.O. 211, that are currently available in the U.S.

3. Expansion of explanation in a few areas, where my teaching experience suggested that this would be helpful.

With these changes, I anticipate that the book will serve beginning navigators in the future as well as it has in the many decades since it was first published.

Thomas C. Bergel
Port Washington, N.Y.
August 1994

Key
to the
Diagrams

The key applies to all the diagrams in this book.

P, P′	North and South Poles
E, E′	Equator
H, H′	Horizon
Q	Center of the Earth
X	Geographical position of the heavenly body under discussion
Z	The observer, or the azimuth angle at the observer
Z′	Observer's zenith
G	Any point on the Greenwich meridian

From the foregoing it follows that:

The line **PZ** is part of the observer's meridian.

The line **PX** is part of the meridian of the geographical position of the heavenly body under discussion.

The line **PG** is part of the Greenwich meridian.

Except where further description is necessary these letters are not explained again in the book.

Abbreviations

DR	Dead reckoning
GHA	Greenwich Hour Angle
GMT	Greenwich Mean Time
UT	Universal Time
GP	Geographical position
IE	Index error
LHA	Local Hour Angle
SD	Semi-diameter
AP	Assumed position
HO	Hydrographic Office (US Naval Oceanographic Office)
Zn	Azimuth
Ha	(Height apparent) Sextant altitude corrected for index error and dip
Hs	(Height sextant) Sextant altitude
Ho	(Height observed) Ha corrected for refraction, semi-diameter and parallax (as necessary)
Hc	(Height calculated) Calculated altitude

The Theory

The Heavenly Bodies

Before the theory of a sight can be understood, there are facts about the Earth you must grasp and terms you must learn.

We navigate by means of the Sun, the Moon, the planets and the stars. Forget how the Earth spins round the Sun with the motionless stars inconceivable distances away; imagine instead that the Earth is the center of the universe and that all the heavenly bodies circle slowly round us, the stars keeping their relative positions while the Sun, Moon and planets change their positions in relation to each other and to the stars. This pre-Copernican outlook comes easily as we watch the heavenly bodies rise and set, and is a help in practical navigation.

The Geographical Position (GP)

At any moment of the day or night there is some spot on the Earth's surface that is directly underneath the Sun. This is the Sun's GP, and it lies where a line drawn from the center of the Earth to the Sun cuts the Earth's surface. It is shown in Fig 1 at X. Not only the Sun but all heavenly bodies have GPs, and these positions can be found from the Almanac at any given moment. The GP is measured by declination and hour angle.

Declination

The declination of a heavenly body is the latitude of its GP, and is measured exactly as latitude is, in degrees north or south of the equator. The Sun's declination moves from 23°N in midsummer when its GP reaches the Tropic of Cancer, to 23°S in midwinter when it reaches the Tropic of Capricorn; in the spring and autumn, at the equinoxes, the declination is 0° as the Sun crosses the equator. The declination of the Sun changes, on average, one degree every four days throughout the year, but the rate of change varies. During the summer solstice in 1990 for example, it takes 34 days for the Sun to climb 1° up and then lose that degree from its peak on midsummer's day: it is indeed well named the solstice (sol = sun, stit = stat as in station). On the other hand, at the equinox, when days and nights are of equal length, the declination changes by two degrees in only five days. Fig 2 shows how declination and latitude are measured as angles at the center of the Earth. Q is the center of the Earth; E a point on the equator immediately north of X; and X, as we have seen, is the GP of the Sun. Since by eye we can see that the Sun is far south, the time of year must be about midwinter.

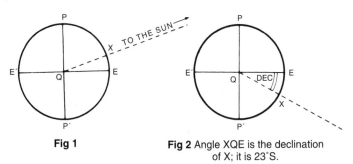

Fig 1

Fig 2 Angle XQE is the declination of X; it is 23°S.

The Moon's declination varies between 28°30'N and S; it changes rapidly, sometimes as much as six or seven degrees in 24 hours. The declinations of the planets change slowly and always lie in a band between 29°N and S. The declinations of the stars are virtually fixed, varying by less than one minute of arc (1') during the year.

The declinations of those heavenly bodies suitable for navigation are found in the Almanac for every hour of the day and can be interpolated to an accuracy of a tenth of a minute (0′.1).

Hour Angle

The GP of any heavenly body is not only on a parallel of latitude but also on a meridian of longitude, and hour angle is the method of measuring this meridian. It differs from longitude in some marked respects.

Let us consider the Sun. You are at the Old Royal Observatory (or anywhere else north of N23°), standing on the Greenwich meridian: when the Sun is due south of you (about noon), its hour angle is nil. Two hours later its hour angle is two hours; and as the Sun sets, goes round to the other side of the Earth and rises again, the hour angle increases until at eleven in the morning it is 23 hours, while at noon it comes the full circle of 24 hours to start again at zero as it crosses the meridian. The hour angle, when it is measured from the Greenwich meridian is called Greenwich Hour Angle (GHA). GHA is always measured in a westerly direction from the meridian of Greenwich to the meridian of the GP of the heavenly body concerned. It can be measured in time or in arc (degrees, minutes and seconds): once round the Earth is 24 hours or 360°.

You might well think that you could tell how far round the Sun had gone since midday and measure hour angle just by looking at an accurate quartz watch, but this is not so. The Sun does not keep regular, or mean, time; it can occasionally be as much as 20 minutes fast or slow on Greenwich Mean Time, so that the GHA of the Sun has to be looked up in the Almanac where it can be found for every hour, minute and second of every day. GMT is now known throughout the world as UT, Universal Time, and will be referred to as such in this book. (It is interesting that since time signals are no longer based on celestial motions but on an atomic time-scale there is a maximum correction of 0.9 of a second to be applied to longitude for those aiming at maximum accuracy—it need not bother us!)

In Fig 3 we are looking down on to the North Pole. The GHA of the Sun is measured west from the Greenwich meridian, as shown by the arrow. It is morning, for the Sun is coming up to

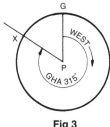

Fig 3

Greenwich and the GHA is approximately 21 hours or 315° (360° = 24h, so 15°= 1 h).

Hour angle can be measured not only from the Greenwich meridian but from any meridian. When it is measured from the meridian on which you, the observer, are standing, it is known as Local Hour Angle (LHA); this, too, is measured in a westerly direction. When you are west of Greenwich, LHA is less than GHA because the Sun passed Greenwich before it passed you, and so GHA is the larger angle. When you are east of Greenwich, LHA is greater than GHA since the Sun passed you first. Whereas GHA is found from the Almanac, LHA is found by adding or subtracting your longitude to, or from, GHA.

(At this point you may well ask: how can I add or subtract my longitude when it is precisely what I am trying to determine? It is a fair question, but just for the moment accept—pretend—that you do know it, and later on you will see why you can make that assumption.)

Consider the examples in Figs 4 through 7. The workings apply not only in the northern hemisphere but also in the southern, indeed from any point on the meridians in question.

EXAMPLE A (FIG 4)

You are somewhere in Canada (Long. 75°W) at 1300 local time. As it is one hour after your noon the Sun will be an hour past your meridian and the LHA (heavy line) will be 1 hour. But it is a long time since the Sun crossed the Greenwich meridian, so the GHA (unbroken line) will be much larger. It will be the 75° of your longitude (broken line) plus the 15° the Sun has gone past you, i.e. 90° (6 hours). In west longitudes:

GHA – observer's longitude = LHA
90°–75°= 15°

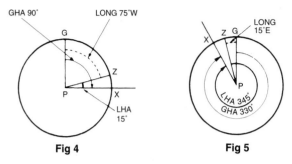

Fig 4   **Fig 5**

EXAMPLE B (FIG 5)

You are in Italy (Long. 15°E) at 1100 local time. Since it is an hour before your noon, LHA (heavy line) is 23 hours or 345°. The Sun has further to go, however, to reach the Greenwich meridian, so GHA (unbroken line) is only 22 hours or 330°. In east longitudes:

GHA + observer's longitude = LHA
330° + 15° = 345°

EXAMPLE C (FIG 6)

You are somewhere in the Atlantic and the Sun has just passed the Greenwich meridian so that GHA is only 1h 30m or 22°30'; but the Sun has not yet reached your meridian PZ (52°30' W). On that meridian it is only 1000 and LHA will be 22 hours or 330°. In spite of this the rule holds good; the observer is west of Greenwich so:

GHA – observer's longitude = LHA

but because the subtraction is impossible as it stands
(22°30' – 52°30') we must add 360° to the GHA to get:

382°30' – 52°30' = 330°

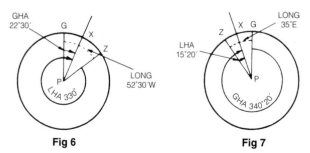

Fig 6   **Fig 7**

EXAMPLE D (FIG 7)

You are in the eastern Mediterranean (Long 35°E). The Sun has passed your meridian but has not yet reached Greenwich. LHA therefore is small but GHA is large, 340°20′ or 22h 41m 20″. Now your longitude is east of Greenwich so:

$$\text{GHA + observer's longitude = LHA}$$
$$340°20′ + 35° = 375°20′$$

When, as here, the resulting figure is more than 360°, 360 must be subtracted from the total, giving LHA 15°20′.
We can now say that:

$$\text{LHA = GHA} \begin{array}{c} + \text{ east} \\ - \text{ west} \end{array} \text{longitude}$$

When, with an easterly longitude, the total comes to more than 360°, that sum (or even occasionally, as we shall see, a multiple of that sum) is subtracted to arrive at LHA. With a westerly longitude, when GHA is less than the observer's longitude, 360° are added to GHA to make the subtraction possible.

These diagrams hold good not only for the Sun but for all heavenly bodies although only the Sun crosses the Greenwich meridian at approximately 12h UT. The daily times of the meridian passages at Greenwich of the Moon and useful planets are given in the Almanac. More importantly, the Almanac tabulates the GHA of those planets, for the Moon and for the "First Point of *Aries*" from which the GHAs of the stars can be calculated (see page 40).

Hour angle differs from longitude in three main ways:

1. HA can be measured in arc or in time (conversion tables are to be found in all almanacs and in many tables); longitude is only measured in arc.
2. HA is always measured in a westerly direction, through 360°; longitude is measured either east or west, through 180°.
3. HA may be:
   (a) GHA, measured from the Greenwich meridian;
   (b) LHA, measured from the meridian of the observer (longitude is always measured from the Greenwich meridian); or
   (c) Sidereal Hour Angle (SHA). (See page 40.)

For any given second, the GHA of any heavenly body useful to navigation can be found in the Almanac and its LHA can be derived by adding or subtracting the longitude of the observer to, or from, GHA.

To return for a moment to the GP, it should now be clear that the GP of any heavenly body is determined by declination and GHA, and that this GP could be plotted on a map (although in fact it is never necessary to do so). As an exercise, try to guess where the GP of the Sun is at the moment you read this. I, for instance, am writing almost on the Greenwich meridian on 17 August at 1635 UT so the Sun passed me 4h 35m ago, its GP lies about longitude 68°W. Its declination and therefore the latitude of its GP, I guess to be N15° (actually N 13°21´, W 67°44´). The sun was over the Caribbean Sea when I started my mental arithmetic, but it travels at a great pace and the plot of its GP is instantly out of date.

The Zenith

If a line were drawn from the center of the Earth through you and out into space, it would lead to your zenith. In other words, it is the point in space immediately above your head. For instance, if you were standing at the GP of the Sun, then the Sun would be in your zenith.

The Horizon

As it is impossible to see round a corner, we cannot see much of the surface of the Earth that bends away from us in all directions. The horizon lies in a plane that at sea level is at a tangent to the

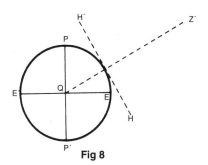

Fig 8

Earth's surface. This plane is at right angles to the direction of the observer's zenith. In Fig 8 HH′ is a tangent to the Earth's surface at Z and both ∠Z′ZH and ∠Z′ZH′ are right angles.

Altitude

The altitude is the angle made at the observer between the Sun (or any other heavenly body) and the horizon directly below it. In Fig 9 ∠HZS is the altitude of the Sun. This is the angle you measure when you take a sight.

Zenith Distance

The zenith distance is the complement of the altitude. In Fig 9 it is ∠Z′ZS.

Altitude + zenith distance = 90°

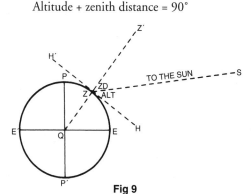

Fig 9

The Elevated Pole

The pole nearer to the observer is called the elevated pole: the North Pole in the northern and the South Pole in the southern hemisphere.

Azimuth and Azimuth Angle

The azimuth is the bearing (true *not* magnetic) of a heavenly body. This bearing may be called azimuth angle (Z) or azimuth (Zn), depending on the method of measurement. Azimuth angle is measured eastwards or westwards from north or south according to the elevated pole: in the northern hemisphere from N to 179°E and from N to 179°W. Azimuth is measured from north through east from 0° to 360°. Fig 10 shows a number of azimuth angles in the northern hemisphere.

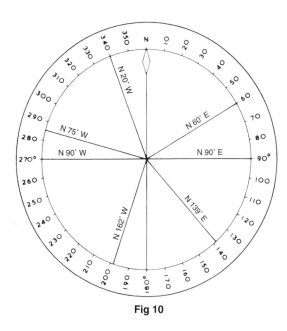

Fig 10

When working out a sight, azimuth is obtained from the tables where a single figure is found; this may be N 145°E or N 145°W depending on whether the heavenly body has passed your meridian or not. For example, in the morning the azimuth angle of the Sun will be N and E, in the afternoon, N and W. To convert the azimuth angle into azimuth, the rule in northern latitudes is:

LHA greater than 180°........... Zn = Z
LHA less than 180°................. Zn = 360° − Z

This rule is given on each page of the tables together with the rule for the southern hemisphere. To take an example, in Lat

N50° with the LHA 22° (afternoon, with the Sun to the west) and Z145°, then:

$$Zn = 360° - 145° = 215°$$

Had you looked along your compass when you took your sight and allowed for magnetic variation, you would have found the Sun on a bearing of 215°. It is never possible, however, to measure azimuth accurately enough with a compass and it must be extracted from the tables.

Great Circles

A great circle is any circle with its center the center of the Earth and its radius the distance from the center to the surface of the Earth. The equator and the meridians are great circles, but the parallels of latitude, except the equator, are not, because the center of a circle formed by a parallel of latitude lies either north or south of the center of the Earth. Distances along a great circle can be measured in two ways: in miles or by the angle subtended at the center of the Earth.

The shortest distance between any two points on the Earth's surface lies along a great circle, and with a globe and a piece of string, you can see roughly where the great circle runs between, say, Glasgow and New York, or Los Angeles and Sydney, by holding one end of the string on one place and pulling it as tight as possible to the other.

In Fig 11 three great circles are shown: EE′, CC′ and the circle PEP′E′ on which A and E lie; AA′ is a parallel of latitude

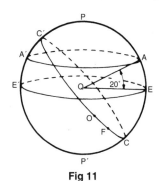

Fig 11

but not a great circle. Since we have said that A and E are on the same meridian, the distance AE can be expressed in two ways: in arc it makes an angle of 20° at Q (the latitude of A is also 20°); in miles, since one minute of arc (1′) subtended at Q makes one nautical mile (1 nm) at the Earth's surface, AE = 20x60 = 1200nm.

CC′ is a great circle (although it is not a meridian, for it does not pass through the poles), and therefore the distance, if known, between O and F, two points on that circle, could also be expressed in miles or arc. These methods of measurement, or of expressing the measurement, can be used between any two points on the Earth's surface, and the interchangeability of arc and mileage should always be kept in mind.

Universal Time (UT)

UT (formerly GMT) is an average, or mean, of the Sun's time, necessary because the Sun rarely crosses the Greenwich meridian at 12h UT, erratically arriving early or late throughout the year. The Almanac gives the "Equation of Time" (E) for midnight and noon daily, showing by how much the Sun differs from UT. The time of the meridian passage alongside tells us if it is fast or slow. For example, at noon on 8 December 1990 (see Appendix A), E is 08m 11s and the meridian passage (to the nearest minute) 11h 52m, telling us that the Sun is over 8 minutes fast on UT.

At this stage, I advise readers to whom all this is new to re-read what has been written so far, because it is important to understand it thoroughly before tackling the next sections.

The Position Line

The final result obtained from any sight on any heavenly body is a straight line on your chart, and you are somewhere on that line. When the Sun is in your zenith its altitude is 90°, and there is only one spot on the Earth's surface where you can be: at the GP of the Sun. As you move away from the GP (or rather as it moves rapidly away from you) the altitude will lessen, and it will lessen equally whether you go north, south, east or west. However far you move you are on a "position circle" with its center at the GP, on which every point is equidistant from the GP

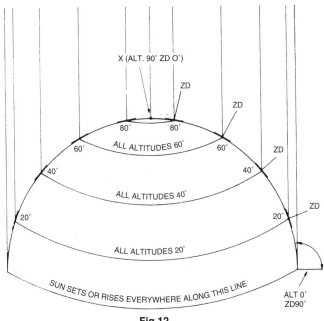

X (ALT. 90° ZD 0°)

ZD

ZD

80° 80°

ALL ALTITUDES 60°

60° 60°

ZD

40° 40°

ALL ALTITUDES 40°

ZD

20° 20°

ALL ALTITUDES 20°

ZD

SUN SETS OR RISES EVERYWHERE ALONG THIS LINE

ALT 0°
ZD90°

Fig 12

and every altitude of the Sun the same. Fig 12 shows how the rays from the Sun, or from any other heavenly body, strike the Earth. The GP is at X and we see that the further the observer is from X the larger the "position circle" and the lower the altitude. The altitude lessens until the Sun disappears below the horizon, when its altitude is 0° and zenith distance 90°.

Fig 13 shows a "position circle" and an azimuth from the observer to the GP; the Sun is to the SW of the observer, who will therefore be on the NE portion of the circle. Unfortunately you cannot obtain the azimuth of the Sun accurately enough to fix your exact position on the circle. The only thing to do is to draw a line at right angles to the most accurate azimuth available and say "I am somewhere on this line." The line is drawn straight because the distance from the center of the circle is so great that it is impossible to show the curve of the circle on the chart.

It may be helpful to realize how very large these "position circles" are. For example, on a winter's morning, when the Sun is over SW Africa, its altitude in England is about 12° and it has

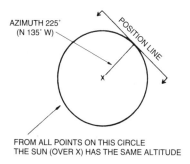

Fig 13

the same altitude in the following places: Greenwich, the Caspian Sea, Madras, the South Pole, Chile, Guyana, and the Azores. Even in midsummer at noon, when the Sun is at its highest (63°) and nearest to England, the circle runs through Greenwich, Istanbul, Cairo, the Congo, the Cape Verde Islands and the Azores.

The fact that the position line is at right angles to the azimuth is of practical value not only for working out sights but also for choosing the best time to take them. In Fig 14 you are approaching a strange coast from the NW and are not certain of your position. A morning sight of the Sun when it bears SE might give you the line AA', determining your distance off the land; while from a sight in the afternoon, line BB' positions you along the coast.

The Meridian Passage

When a heavenly body crosses the meridian of the observer, either to the north or to the south of him, an excellent opportunity occurs for an easy sight, for two reasons. First, no plotting is required. A position line, as we have seen, lies at right angles to the bearing of the heavenly body under observation, so when the body crosses your meridian, i.e. is due north or south of you, your position line will run east and west, and a line running east and west is a parallel of latitude. Secondly, accurate time is not required because the moment of passage is when the altitude of the body is at its highest. Such observations are most commonly

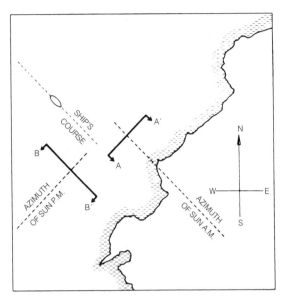

Fig 14

used for the Sun—a "noon sight"—and for *Polaris*, the Pole Star, which is more or less permanently on everyone's meridian to the north.

There are four cases, similar in principle:

CASE 1, FIG 15

Every heavenly body is so far from the Earth that its rays strike the Earth in parallel lines (but see page 21), a band of light rather than a cone as was shown in Fig 12. In Fig 15, PZXP' is the meridian on which both Z and X lie. Two parallel rays from the Sun, SZ and S'XQ, hit the meridian at Z and X, and cross the straight line Z'ZQ. It follows that $\angle Z'ZS$ and $\angle ZQX$ are equal. Now $\angle Z'ZS$ is the zenith distance, so when we observe the altitude of the Sun we learn the size of this angle ($90° - Alt = ZD$). From the Almanac we can find $\angle XQE$ for it is the declination. Add $\angle ZQX$ and $\angle XQE$ and the resulting $\angle ZQE$ is the latitude of Z.

Latitude = Zenith Distance + Declination
LAT = ZD + DEC

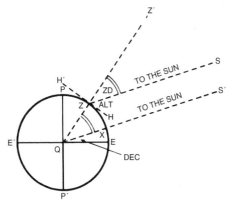

Fig 15

CASE 2, FIG 16

The observer at Z is taking a noon sight of the Sun (at X and on the same meridian). X is south of the equator so the declination is south, and we can see here that ∠ZQX includes ∠EQX and so the latitude of Z = ∠ZXQ – ∠EQX; that is, Latitude = Zenith Distance – Declination.

$$\text{LAT} = \text{ZD} - \text{DEC}$$

When declination and latitude are both north or both south the situation is known as *same name*; when one is north and the other south it is called *contrary name*. We can therefore say, in Cases 1

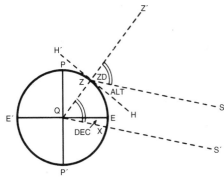

Fig 16

and 2 where the observer is between the body observed (here the Sun) and the elevated pole, that:

$$\text{Latitude} = \text{Zenith Distance} \begin{array}{l} + \text{(same name)} \\ - \text{(contrary name)} \end{array} \text{Declination}$$
$$\text{LAT} = \text{ZD} \pm \text{DEC}$$

CASE 3, FIG 17

The third case is where the GP of the body observed is between the observer and the elevated pole. Once again $\angle Z'ZS = \angle ZQX$. $\angle XQE$, the declination, consists of $\angle ZQX + ZQE$, the observer's latitude, so:

$$\text{Latitude} = \text{Declination} - \text{Zenith Distance}$$
$$\text{LAT} = \text{DEC} - \text{ZD}$$

Observations of Polaris present good examples of this configuration and are useful because, as with other meridian sights, accurate time is not necessary while the star is always available, only a few minor corrections being required to adjust for its not being precisely over the North Pole.

CASE 4, FIG 18

One further case occurs, mainly in far northern or southern latitudes, when the observer and the GP of the body observed are on opposite sides of the elevated pole: then

$$L = 180° - (\text{DEC} + \text{ZD})$$

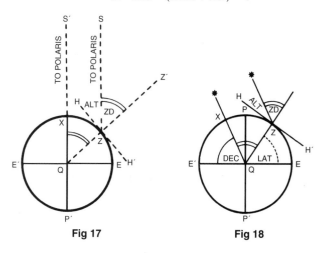

Fig 17　　　　　**Fig 18**

Spherical Triangles

We have seen that in each of the last four diagrams the zenith distance is equal to the angle subtended at the Earth's center by the observer and the GP. This is true not only of noon sights or observations of *Polaris*, when the GP is due north or south of the observer, but of all sights, whatever the bearing of the heavenly body. The zenith distance *always* equals the angle at the Earth's center made by the GP and the observer. Looking again at Figs 15–18, ∠ZQX will always equal ZD even when the two points Z and X no longer lie on a meridian but on some other great circle. This angle can be translated into miles at the Earth's surface: an altitude of 47° gives a zenith distance of 43° which, since 1' of arc = 1nm, means that the GP is 43x60 = 2580 miles away from the observer.

We now know that by taking a sight and finding the zenith distance we can find our distance from the GP of any visible body (provided its particulars are tabled in the Almanac), but because the distances involved are so huge, we cannot put a compass on the GP and draw the required circle. Nor can we mark the position line on our charts except when the body is on our meridian and the distances are conveniently marked by parallels of latitude.

We must therefore approach the problem from a different direction. We pretend that we do not know the altitude of the heavenly body (although we have just measured it) but that we *do* know where we are. We assume we know our latitude and longi-

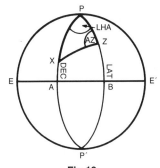

Fig 19

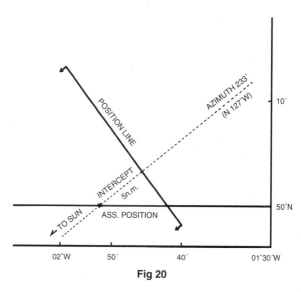

Fig 20

tude and we work from an *assumed position* (often abbreviated AP).

In Fig 19 we are looking at the outside of the Earth; PAP′ and PBP′ are the meridians of X and Z crossing the equator at A and B. What do we know about the triangle PZX? We know the length of the d PZ; BZ is the observer's (assumed) latitude, therefore:

$$PZ = 90° - \text{Latitude of observer}$$

We know the length of the side PX; AX is the declination, therefore:

$$PX = 90° - \text{Declination of heavenly body observed}$$

We know the size of the included angle ZPX, since this is the local hour angle (the angle between the observer's meridian and the meridian of the GP measured in a westerly direction).

Now if we know two sides and the included angle of a triangle, we can by means of spherical trigonometry, or by tables, find out the length of the side XZ and the other two angles. The length of the side XZ is equal to the zenith distance, so that Altitude = 90°− XZ. This is called the *calculated altitude*, abbreviated Hc. Had we taken a perfect sight at our assumed position at that particular time we should have got the same figure from our sextant—the observed altitude (see page 20).

The Intercept

Imagine that we take a sight of the Sun with an observed altitude of 41°38′ from the sextant. We know we are somewhere southwest of the Isle of Wight, and we assume that our position is N50°00′ W01°54′ (the reasons why we choose this position rather than another will become apparent later). After the necessary calculations, we get a calculated altitude from the tables of 41°43′. If we had been at the assumed position, our observed altitude also would have been 41°43′, but it was not, so we are somewhere else. The difference between the calculated altitude and the observed altitude is 5′ and, since 5′ = 5nm, our position line will be 5 miles away from the assumed position. This is called an *intercept* of 5 miles. The intercept should not be greater than 45′; if it is, you should use a different assumed position.

If you look again at Fig 19 you will see that ∠PZX is the azimuth that can now be estimated. For the sight we have just taken, the tables tell us that the azimuth angle Z was 127°, and because it was afternoon we know this was N127°W (Zn 233°). We now mark our assumed position on the chart (Fig 20) and draw the azimuth through it. As has already been explained, the position line lies at right angles to the azimuth, the intercept was 5 miles, so, from our assumed position, our position line will be 5nm *away* from or *towards* the Sun. The farther we move away from the GP the less the altitude, so if our observed altitude was less than our calculated altitude we must have been farther away than we assumed. In this case the calculated altitude was 41°43′, the observed altitude 41°38′, so the position line will be away

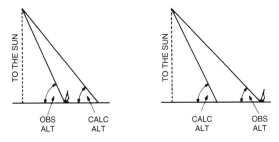

Fig 21 Calculated altitude greater...AWAY
Calculated altitude less...TOWARDS

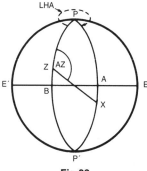

Fig 22

from the Sun. The position line can be drawn, as shown, with little arrows pointing towards the body observed, which helps to stop you making a mistake. Fig 21 shows the principle of the intercept schematically.

Fig 22 shows another example of the triangle that must always be solved. Here X is the GP of the Sun. From merely looking at this triangle we can tell certain things: it is morning at Z, for the Sun is to the east, and it is winter for the Sun's declination is south of the equator. Now PZ = 90° – Latitude of the observer; PX = 90° + Declination, and ∠ZPX = LHA. In this case LHA, measured west from the meridian of Z, is (say) 323° and the internal angle (ZPX) is 360°– 323° = 37°; but the tables will look after all that for us and the important point is that we know the size of the angle. ZX and ∠PZX can now be calculated and the calculated altitude (90° – ZX) and the azimuth angle found in the tables.

This is the principle of every sight taken—that with the known facts about a heavenly body and an assumed position we can calculate an altitude, and that the more the calculated altitude differs from the observed altitude, the further the position line moves from the assumed position (always remaining perpendicular to the azimuth line).

Sextant Altitude and Observed Altitude

When you take a sight, the angle you read off from your sextant is called the sextant altitude (Hs), to which certain corrections must be applied to obtain observed altitude (Ho). It is observed altitude that is compared with the calculated altitude (Hc).

Dip (height of eye) The calculated altitude derived from the tables is given as if you were at sea level, but at sea your eye may be 6 or 60 feet above it depending on whether you are in a yacht or a liner. The correction must be made to the sextant altitude to make it a sea-level reading; in small boats it is usually about –3ʹ. It must be applied to all sights except those taken with a bubble sextant or an artificial horizon.

Refraction Just as a pencil appears to bend when you put it in a glass of water, the rays of light from heavenly bodies are bent, or refracted, when passing through the Earth's atmosphere. The lower the altitude of the body, the greater is the refraction. Sights below 6° are inadvisable and those below 10° should be treated with caution. A correction for refraction must be applied to all sights.

Semi-Diameter (Fig 23) This correction applies only to the Sun and Moon. In theory, when taking a sight, the horizon should bisect the "body," but this is impractical and when observing the Sun the bottom or lower limb is usually rested on the horizon; the Sun's *upper* limb can be used if the lower limb is hidden by clouds. With the Moon, the limb used depends on which is available. In each case half the diameter of the body must be allowed for. Semi-diameter is given in the Almanac every three days for both Sun and Moon. The correction, usually about 16ʹ, is added for the lower and subtracted for the upper; but not with a bubble sextant or artificial horizon.

Parallax It was said earlier that the rays from heavenly bodies strike the Earth in parallel. This is not strictly true, but as far as the Sun, stars and planets are concerned the parallax correction is negligible and can be ignored. The Moon, however, is so much nearer to the Earth that a considerable correction is often necessary. The maximum value of this correction occurs when the

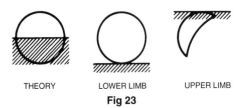

THEORY   LOWER LIMB   UPPER LIMB

Fig 23

Moon is on the horizon (altitude zero). This value is called *horizontal parallax* (HP), and is tabulated in the *Nautical Almanac*. The correction for altitudes above the horizon is called *parallax in altitude* (PA). It is not tabulated as such in the Almanac, but is incorporated into the Altitude Correction Tables for the Moon. (For those mathematically inclined, PA equals HP times the cosine of the altitude.)

The navigator who uses the *Nautical Almanac* need not be concerned with refraction, semi-diameter and parallax as such. The Almanac has separate Altitude Correction Tables for the Sun, for Stars and Planets, and for the Moon. Each of these tables incorporates all the corrections required for that body: refraction plus semi-diameter for the Sun, refraction alone for Stars and Planets, and refraction plus semi-diameter plus parallax for the Moon.

The Practice

Almanacs and Tables

The practice of working out a sight can be broken down into two distinct parts: first, locating the position of the body observed at that particular moment on that particular day in that year when you took your sight, information that must come from an almanac; and, secondly, reducing the spherical triangle so found, for which tables or a calculator are necessary. Any almanac (including one stored in a calculator) can be used with any tables and vice versa, although certain tables and almanacs are designed to be used together. Most calculators can replace tables, some resolving the triangle more easily than others.

ALMANACS

These are published annually, and the one for the current year must be used. They give the positions (GHA and declination) of the heavenly bodies throughout the year, as well as additional information such as times of sunrise and sunset, eclipses, the Moon's phases, etc.

The *Nautical Almanac*, used for the examples in this book, is published in one volume for the year; it is designed for marine use and gives the required information in a compact and simple way. It has a section to help those using calculators, and also a set of tables (new in 1990) called "Concise Sight Reduction Tables" that, although more complex than those used for the examples in this book, allows a sailor to dispense with any other tables.

The *Air Almanac*, as its title implies, is designed for use in aircraft. It is tabulated at smaller intervals of time than the *Nautical Almanac*, and was formerly issued in three volumes per year, each covering four months. It is now issued only as one large and rather expensive volume that covers the entire year. It is therefore little used at present, and has become hard to find. It is easy to use, and if you do find one you will have no difficulty in adapting from the *Nautical Almanac*.

SIGHT REDUCTION TABLES

These are mathematical tables that never go out of date, with the one exception of H. O. 249 Vol 1, which covers only nine years. Modern tables are entered with LHA, declination and latitude to find tabulated altitude and azimuth. They solve the innumerable variations of the spherical triangle. (For pure interest, H.O. 229 has 720 solutions to a full page, 360 pages to a volume and six volumes, giving precalculated solutions of more than one-and-a-half million different spherical triangles.) Several sets of tables are available for the yacht navigator.

Sight Reduction Tables for Air Navigation (H.O. 249) are the tables used for the examples in this book. They consist of three volumes:

> Vol 1 Selected Stars (Epoch 1995.0)
> Vol 2 Latitudes 0°–39°, Declinations 0°–29°
> Vol 3 Latitudes 40°–89°, Declinations 0°–29°

Sight Reduction Tables for Marine Navigation (H.O. 229) are designed for use with the *Nautical Almanac*. The tables consist of six volumes, each covering 16° of latitude and declinations from 0°–90°. They are more precise (tabulated to 0.1′) and more comprehensive (covering all declinations, to 90°) than H.O. 249. A full set is rather bulky and expensive, and their greater precision is of no particular advantage in yacht navigation. They replaced H.O. 214, of which many copies are still in use. Those navigators used to H.O. 249 will have no problems in adapting to either H.O. 229 or H.O. 214 if they want to change.

"Short" Tables are very compact tables, not precalculated like those mentioned above, but designed to enable the navigator to fairly easily calculate the solution to any spherical triangle. They include the "Concise Sight Reduction Tables" now incorporated into the Nautical Almanac, but several others are also available. They are briefly described on page 51 in the "Notes" section of this book.

A Sun Sight In Winter

USING THE SEXTANT

Let us pretend you are in the North Sea, DR position N51°56′, E1°51′, on the morning of 7 December 1990, and that you wish to take a sun sight.

In order to work out your sight, you need two things: the sextant altitude of the Sun and the exact time at which you measured that altitude. So far we have looked at the various examples as if we had been able to stop the movement of the heavens and examine each situation at leisure, but, unlike Joshua, we cannot make the Sun stand still or stay the Moon; all is in continual movement, so that every answer is valid for an infinitesimal period only and we can but try to time it as best we can. The extent of an error in time varies considerably. In the arc-into-time conversion table we see that 1′ = 4s, so that at the worst, an error of four seconds could make a difference of one nautical mile; thus a watch misread by a minute could cause an error of 15 miles. It is hardly ever as bad as this, for the heavenly body must be due east or west of you to cause the maximum effect, but a mistake of 1° of LHA (4 minutes) can easily put you 45 miles out.

Do not try at first to take your own time: get someone else to do it for you—and make sure he can tell the time, particularly if he is using an analog watch. It is quite amazing how many people there are who, when you say "now," do not write down the correct time.

Take your sextant and make yourself comfortable, well supported and firm from the waist down, mobile from the waist up. Make sure that you have a clear view of the Sun and of the horizon below it. Generally, the higher up you are the better, because it is easier to avoid false horizons made by wave tops, but it is not worth making yourself unsteady to gain height. It is also, obviously, important to choose a place where there is a minimum of spray. Arrange your shade glasses so that you have a bright Sun but not one that will dazzle you; use a pale horizon glass to remove glare when necessary.

The clarity of the horizon is of the greatest importance. Sometimes in calms, there is not enough difference between air and water to distinguish the horizon; on other occasions mist obscures the true horizon, giving a false horizon closer to you. Very rarely there may be abnormal dip (refraction), which can be recognized by the appearance of "boiling" on the horizon or by the funnels of distant ships seeming to reach up into the sky. When you have doubts about the reliability of the horizon, if it looks in any way odd or hazy, either avoid sights or treat your results with great caution.

RECORDING THE SIGHTS

When you have the Sun more or less on the horizon, rock the sextant gently from side to side and you will see the Sun swing as if it were attached to a pendulum; it is at the lowest point of this swing that you take the sight. Adjust the sextant and, when you feel sure that the Sun is just brushing the horizon, call to your timekeeper and then read off to him the degrees and minutes from your sextant. How accurately you read your sights depends in part on the sextant: some read to 0'.1, others to 0'.5. Readings to the nearest half minute of arc are quite adequate to start with. Take a series of five sights at about 40-second intervals; they will appear something like the example below.

SUN, Friday 7 December 1990

Watch			Sextant	
h	m	s		
10	54	31	14°	31.0
10	55	56	14	32.4
10	56	37	14	36.9
10	57	34	14	33.5
10	58	12	14	38.4
	5)280	170	5)172.2	
10	56	34	14°	34'.4

You will notice that in this series the Sun is rising, indeed it is still an hour to noon, but it is rising very slowly so that a small error in the observations can make it appear that the Sun is already sinking (look at reading number 4). In spring and autumn the change in altitude will be much more marked. The object of averaging five sights is to compensate for these little mistakes. If you can only take three sights, average them, but do not rely on the position line from a single observation.

CORRECTING THE DATA

Now with a watch time of 10h 56m 34s and a sextant altitude of 14°34′.4 you can start to work out your sight. The relevant pages of the *Nautical Almanac* are reproduced as Appendix A.

Watch time to UT (GMT)

	h	m	s	
Watch	10	56	34	(The watch is here assumed to be on UT
Corr.			−5	and 5s fast.)
UT	10	56	29	

Sextant Altitude to Observed Altitude   As we saw earlier, the sextant altitude must be corrected. The first correction is for index error, the error of your sextant (see page 48). In this example an imaginary error of 2′.3 "off" is allowed for. The other corrections are found in the *Nautical Almanac* in the Altitude Correction Tables on the first two pages for the Sun, stars and planets, and at the end for the Moon (see Appendices D and E). Under "Dip," presuming a height of eye above sea level of between 9 and 10 ft, we find a correction of minus 3′.0. In the Sun column "Oct – Mar, Lower Limb," against our sextant altitude 14°34′ (between 14°18′ and 14°42′) we find plus 12′.6. This last correction includes both refraction and semi-diameter, so we have:

Sextant	14° 34′.4
IE	+ 2 .3
Dip	− 3 .0
Alt. Corr.	+ 12 .6
Observed Alt	14° 46′ (to the nearest minute)

This is the figure that will be compared with the calculated altitude.

Note: The Altitude Correction Tables in the *Nautical Almanac* should theoretically be entered with *apparent* altitude (sextant altitude corrected for index error and dip), but this is unnecessarily precise for anything except possibly the Moon, and sextant altitude can be used instead.

USING THE ALMANAC

LHA Sun from UT   Each double page in the main body of the *Nautical Almanac* provides the necessary data for three days: on the left, the GHA of *Aries*, the GHA and declination of Venus, Mars, Jupiter and Saturn, and the Sidereal Hour Angles and declinations of 57 stars; on the right, the GHAs and declinations of Sun and Moon and the times of twilight, sunrise and sunset, moonrise and moonset. GHA SUN is tabulated for every hour and at 10 hours on 7 December 1990 is 332°09′.7, leaving 56m 29s of our chosen UT unaccounted for (Appendix A). The figure to be added to GHA for these minutes and seconds is called the *increment*.

At the back of the *Nautical Almanac* there are 30 yellow pages headed "Increments and Corrections." These consist of 60 tables, one for each minute through the hour. They do not change from year to year. Appendix C shows the page for 56m and 57m. Three columns (Sun/Planets, *Aries*, Moon) give the (very similar) figures that must be added to the hourly figure of GHA. In the 56m Sun column, against 29s we find 14°07′.3, the increment to be added to GHA SUN for 10h to give GHA SUN at the moment we made our observation, namely 10h 56m 29s. The working looks like this:

GHA SUN (10h)	332° 09′.7
Increment (56m 29s)	+ 14° 07′.3
GHA SUN	346° 17′

Now the included angle of the spherical triangle was not GHA but LHA, and when discussing hour angles we saw that LHA equals GHA plus or minus longitude. One way to remember which to do is by the old rhyme:

> Longitude east, GHA least,
> Longitude west, GHA best.

In our case DR longitude is east, so you must add it to get

LHA. Personally, I remember the words "East Add" and write them on any form and any almanac I use. Obviously, west requires the opposite sign.

USING THE TABLES

Assuming a Position   It is necessary at this point to explain the "assumed position." In the past the spherical triangle was resolved by the Cosine-Haversine method and the sight was worked out from the DR position; today it is also easy to use the DR position when working with a computer. Tables, however, cannot print solutions for every minute of arc of latitude, LHA and declination, so the problem is simplified by providing tables only for whole degrees of latitude and LHA. The following three rules determine which position you will assume:

1 Your assumed position must be as near your DR position as possible.
2 Your assumed latitude must be a whole number of degrees.
3 Your assumed longitude must be so arranged as to make your LHA a whole number of degrees.

Rules 1 and 2 are simple and need no explanation; rule 3 is a little more complicated and two imaginary cases are given below:

(a) DR Long E	08° 25′		
	GHA	337°01′	
	Ass Long E	7°59′	(E+)
	LHA	345°00′	
(b) DR Long W	04° 50′		
	GHA	27°32′	
	Ass Long W	4°32′	(E+)
	LHA	23°00′	

To return to our sight, DR Longitude is E 001°51′ so to get LHA we have:

	GHA	346°17′.0	
	Ass Long E	1°43′.0	(E+)
	LHA	348°00′.0	

As has been said, the assumed latitude must be an integral degree, and since the DR latitude was N51°56′, the assumed latitude will be N52°.

Declination   From the same page in the Almanac (Appendix A), write down the Sun's declination for 10h (S 22°36′.1) and also note the value of *d* given at the bottom of the column (0′.3). This figure is the difference in declination during one hour; for the Sun a mean figure is tabulated for every three days. Near the solstices, *d* is very small. Turning to the "56m" table (Appendix C), we will now use the right-hand half, the 3 columns headed "*v* or *d* corr." These 3 columns actually form one long table, which applies for the whole minute (no seconds required) and which give the correction (for the minute) when *v* or *d* (for a whole hour) is 0.0′ to 18.0′. In this case, the *d* of 0.3′ gives a *d*-correction which is also 0.3′ (because 56m is so close to one hour). The sign (+ or −) for *d* is found by inspection of the declination column: when the declination is increasing, the correction must be added; when decreasing, subtracted. For example, the *d*-correction for the Sun will be added from 21 March to 22 June while the declination increases from 0° to N23°, and again from 21 September to 22 December (0° to S23°), but it must be subtracted from 22 June to 21 September (N23° to 0°) and from 22 December to 21 March (S23° to 0°).

It is worth noting that 1 nautical mile is the maximum error that can arise even if the *d*-correction for the Sun is ignored altogether.

Calculated Altitude and Azimuth   We have now found the three arguments necessary for entering H. O. 249: LHA, Declination and Assumed Latitude. In our example:

LHA 348° Dec S22°36′.4 Ass Lat N52°

In H. O. 249, Vol 3, turn to Latitude 52°, which takes up eight pages with four headings:

> Declination 0°–14° *same* name as latitude
> Declination 0°–14° *contrary* name to latitude
> Declination 15°–29° *same* name as latitude
> Declination 15°–29° *contrary* name to latitude

"Name" refers to "north" and "south" and in our example we must look under *contrary* name because declination is south and latitude north (Appendix F).

Each degree of declination has three columns: the tabulated altitude Hc, the difference *d*, and the azimuth angle Z. (*d* is the difference between the tabulated altitudes for one degree of declination and for the next higher degree and determines what proportion of the minutes of declination are to be added or subtracted from Hc.)

Tabular entry should *always* be for the integral degree of declination numerically *less* than (or equal to) the actual declination. The excess over the integral degree, i.e., the minutes and tenths of minutes of the declination, are called the declination increment. For example, with a declination of 12°50′ the tables will be entered with 12° and the declination increment is 50′.

In our example, declination is 22°36′ (to the nearest minute of arc) so 22° is used as argument and 36′ is the declination increment. Against LHA 348° we read: Hc 15°16′, *d*60, Z169°. Now this altitude is correct for 22° declination, but is still to be corrected for the declination increment. At the back of H. O. 249 (and also on a loose card) you will find "Table 5—Correction to Tabulated Altitude for Minutes of Declination" (Appendix G). Under *d*60 and against 36 you find 36 again (it will not be the same figure when *d* is not 60). These 36 minutes must now be subtracted (subtracted because *d* was preceded by a minus sign) from 15°16′ to get the correct calculated altitude:

$$Hc = 15°16′ − 36′ = 14°40′$$

The last figure from the tables, under Z, is the azimuth angle, and since the Sun has not yet passed your meridian it is N169°E, and the azimuth (Zn) is also 169°. This can be confirmed by the instructions in the top corner of the page of the tables where it states: "N Lat, LHA greater than 180°...Zn = Z."

PLOTTING THE SIGHT

Now the observed altitude was 14°46′ and the calculated altitude is less by 6′ or 6 nautical miles. This intercept will be marked "towards" the Sun because the observed altitude is the greater (see

Fig 24

Sight Reduction by H.O. 249 Vols II,III

Date: _7 Dec 1990_ DR Lat: _N 51° 56'_
Body: _SUN LL_ DR Long: _E 01° 51'_
Time: _10:56:29 UT_ AP Lat: _N 52°_

GHA: _332° 09.7'_	v:	HP:
Increment: _14° 07.3'_		
v-corr:		

GHA: _346° 17.0'_	
AP Long: _01° 43.0'_	(E+)
LHA: _348°_	

Declination: _S 22° 36.1'_ d: _+0.3'_
d-corr: _+ 0.3'_

Declination: _S 22° 36.4'_

H tabulated: _15° 16'_ d: _−60_ Z: _169°_
Corr. for ': _− 36'_

Hc: _14° 40'_

Corrections: Moon:
Hs: _14° 34.4'_ 1)
IE: _+ 02.3'_ 2)
Dip: _− 03.0'_ UL

Ha: _14° 33.7'_
Corr: _+ 12.6'_ ←

Ho: _14° 46'_
Hc: _14° 40'_

Intercept: _06' TOWARD_ Zn: _169°_

Fig 21). If you think about moving towards the Sun, it will get higher and the altitude angle greater. In practice, I advise writing *calculated greater away* where you can easily see it and go by rule of thumb.

You are now ready to put the position line on the chart (Fig 25). Mark in the assumed position, draw the azimuth from it (be careful to take it from the true, not the magnetic, rose), mark off 6 miles towards the Sun, draw a line at right angles to the azimuth and there you are!

In case this seems very complicated, Fig 24 shows the workings without explanations: eight small additions or subtractions.

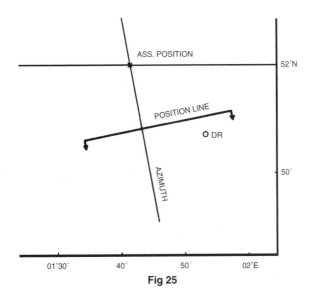

Fig 25

A Sun Sight in Summer

Fig 26 shows another Sun sight taken in July; the relevant page of the *Nautical Almanac* is reproduced in Appendix B.

You will notice that this second sight differs very little from the first; the assumed longitude is subtracted because "Longitude west, GHA best"; declination and latitude are both north so we look under "Declination *same* name as Latitude" in H. O. 249. Fig 28 shows this sight plotted together with that of the Moon given as an example in the next section.

A Moon Sight

Moon sights are as easy to take as Sun sights and almost as easy to work out; they can also be extremely useful. For example, when the Moon is waning and visible in the morning sky, a simultaneous Sun and Moon sight (that is one Sun and one Moon sight taken within a few minutes of each other) gives you two position lines and therefore a fix.

The principle of a Moon sight is exactly the same as that of

Fig 26

Sight Reduction by H.O. 249 Vols II,III

Date:	*17 July 1990*	DR Lat:	*N 40° 09'*	
Body:	*Sun LL*	DR Long:	*W 20° 08'*	
Time:	*10:03:12 UT*	AP Lat:	*N 40°*	

GHA:	*328° 28.5'*	v:		HP:
Increment:	*48.0'*			
v-corr:				

GHA:	*329° 16.5'*		
AP Long:	*20° 16.5'*	(E+)	

LHA:	*309°*

Declination:	*N 21° 12.6'*	d:	*− 0.4'*
d-corr:	*0.0'*		

Declination:	*N 21° 12.6'*

H tabulated:	*42° 53'*	d:	*+ 34*	Z:	*098°*
Corr. for ':	*+ 07'*				

Hc:	*43° 00'*

Corrections:		Moon:
Hs:	*43° 06.7'*	1)
IE:	*−02'*	2)
Dip:	*−03'*	UL

Ha:	*43° 01.7'*	
Corr:	*+ 15.0'*	←

Ho:	*43° 17'*
Hc:	*43° 00'*

Intercept:	*17' TOWARD*	Zn:	*098°*

a Sun sight, but because the Moon moves very irregularly and is much closer to the Earth, the corrections to be applied are more, and more complicated. For each day, in the Moon section of the *Nautical Almanac* (Appendix A) there are five columns which, for each hour, give:

GHA   This is taken out for the hour, and the appropriate increment for minutes and seconds added, as for the Sun.

v   The increment for the Moon is tabulated for the lowest rate of change per hour, but the Moon often moves much faster and a correction is necessary for this *variation*.

Fig 27

Sight Reduction by H.O. 249 Vols II, III

Date: *17 July 1990* DR Lat: *N 40° 09'*
Body: *MOON UL* DR Long: *W 20° 08'*
Time: *09:57:14 UT* AP Lat: *N 40°*

GHA: *023° 52.0'*	v: *5.7*	HP: *59.8*
Increment: *013° 39.4'*		
v-corr: *05.5'*		
GHA: *037° 36.9'*		
AP Long: *020° 36.9'*	(E+)	
LHA: *017°*		
Declination: *N 22° 41.3'*	d: *+9.2'*	
d-corr: *+ 8.8'*		
Declination: *N 22° 50.1'*		
H tabulated: *66° 56'*	d: *+49*	Z: *136°*
Corr. for ': *+ 41'*		
Hc: *67° 37'*		

Corrections:		Moon:
Hs: *67° 10.6'*	1) *+32.6'*
IE: *– 02.0'*	2) *+ 03.8'*
Dip: *– 03.0'*	UL *– 30.0'*
Ha: *67° 05.6'*	*+06.4'*
Corr: *+ 06.4'*	←
Ho: *67° 12'*	
Hc: *67° 37'*	
Intercept: *25' AWAY*	Zn: *224°*

Dec   Declination is tabulated for every hour as for the Sun.

d   The *difference* is given for each hour for the Moon instead of every three days for the Sun. The sign (+ or –) must be found by inspection of the declination, as it was for the Sun.

HP   The value of horizontal parallax (see page 22) is used for entering the second section of the Altitude Correction Tables for the Moon (Appendix E).

Let us look at an example: if a Moon sight were taken at

UT 07h 56m 01s and for the day and hour we find the value of v to be 6'.2 and that of d to be 12'.9 then from "Increments and Corrections" (Appendix C) we get an increment of 13°22'.0, v 5'.8, d 12'.1. The v and d correction columns are valid for the entire minute and no account is to be taken of the seconds of UT. The v correction for the Moon is always additive; the sign for d will depend on the behaviour of the Moon's declination (just as it did for that of the Sun). Neither v nor d can be ignored for the Moon.

Usually you can choose by eye which limb of the Moon to observe, only when it is nearly full is this not so. However, the Almanac does not print the data necessary for a theoretical answer, so go by rule of thumb—waxing upper, waning lower—remembering that, in these rather special circumstances, there may be an error. It is not likely to be more than a mile or so.

Sextant altitude to observed altitude is also rather more complicated for the Moon than it was for the Sun. Correct the sextant altitude for index error and dip to arrive at apparent altitude, and with this figure as argument enter the tables at the back of the *Nautical Almanac* (Appendix E). It is superfluous to discuss here the clear instructions given there; here are two examples:

required data	App Alt	33°42'	49°36'
	HP	57'.6	61'.5
	Limb (U or L)	upper	lower
corrections	1st corr	57'.2	47'.2
	2nd corr	3.6	8.6
		60.8	
	Upper Limb	−30.0	
	Total corr	+30'.8	+55'.8

In the past the Moon was considered unreliable for observations, probably owing to difficulties with the complicated interpolations that were required for such a fast-moving body. Modern almanacs make it possible to reduce lunar observations quickly and with all the necessary accuracy.

Fig 27 shows a Moon sight taken a few minutes before the summer Sun sight; the chartwork is shown in Fig 28 and gives a fix.

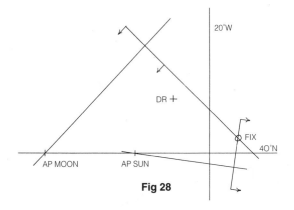

Fig 28

A Running Fix

A simultaneous Sun/Moon fix is very desirable when it is possible, but these two bodies are in the necessary relationship only for a few days each month, so you cannot count on this for your everyday routine. What you can do every day (weather permitting) is to get what is called a "running fix," which is based on two Sun sights taken a few hours apart.

Suppose again that the date is 17 July 1990, but that the Moon does *not* happen to be in a convenient position. (In fact, on the same date in 1994, the Sun will be in almost exactly the same position, but the position of the Moon will be altogether different.) Now take a Sun sight, wait a few hours for the azimuth of the Sun to change significantly (say 45° or more), and then take, work out and plot a second Sun sight. Then you must replot, or "advance," the position line from the earlier sight, taking account of the movement of the vessel between the times of the two sights. The two Sun sights should preferably be spaced about equally before and after noon, since this will give the least elapsed time for a given change of azimuth. Ideally, the sights would be taken when the bearing of the Sun is about 135° (SE) and about 225° (SW), in order to give position lines that cross at about 90°.

Your morning DR position is N 40° 10', W 19° 43'. Local noon will be at about 1320 UT. When the Sun bears SE, you take the first sight, at UT 11:52:37, obtaining an Ho of 62°

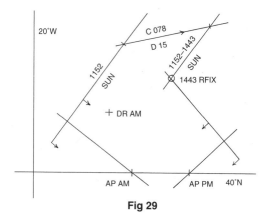

Fig 29

37.8'. This is worked out and plotted (AP N 40°, W 19° 37.8', Zn 127°, intercept 14 AWAY). When the Sun bears SW, you take the second sight, at UT 14:43:47, obtaining an Ho of 64° 28.8'. This is worked out and plotted (AP N 40°, W 19° 25.1', Zn 228°, intercept 8 AWAY). Your DR indicates that, in the time between the sights, you have travelled 15 nautical miles on a course of 078° true. On your plot, draw a line at a bearing of 078° through *any* point on the position line from the first sight. Measure off 15 nautical miles along the 78 degree line, from the first position line. Through the resulting point, draw the advanced line parallel to the original line. You have now, in effect, dead-reckoned from *every* point on the original line; if you were *anywhere* on the original line, you are now *somewhere* on the advanced line. The intersection of the second line and the advanced first line is the running fix (Fig 29).

Planet Sights

There is nearly always a planet handy for observing in the early morning or evening. A planet is brighter than a star and can therefore be used when the horizon is more easily visible. Four columns in the *Nautical Almanac* give the data for Venus, Mars, Jupiter and Saturn. Values for *v* and *d* are given at the bottom of each column, each figure being a mean for three days: these corrections are quite small, except for Saturn when an error of (maximum) 2′.7 could be introduced into your calculations by ignoring the corrections. The only difference from Sun and Moon sights is that v is sometimes a minus quantity for Venus. The corrections to be applied to sextant altitude are given on pages A2 and A3 of the *Nautical Almanac* (see Appendix D). Index error and dip must be applied as always and the altitude correction is for refraction only, as semi-diameter is not, of course, required.

A diagram in the *Nautical Almanac* displays the movement of the planets throughout the year. Very clear notes on the visibility of each planet and on the use of the diagram allow one to identify each planet, an interesting exercise even when you have no intention of taking a sight. Finally, the notes include a section headed "Do not confuse" to help when two planets are close together. If, in spite of this, you find that you are sailing briskly through Pittsburgh, it is quite probable that you have mistaken your planet or even observed a bright star.

Meridian Sights

A meridian sight of the Sun is usually called "a noon sight" because it is taken at the observer's local noon. When taking a noon sight, the first step is to discover the time the Sun will cross your meridian. The time of the Sun's meridian passage at Greenwich is given for each day at the bottom of the right-hand page of the Nautical Almanac (that of the Moon is also given). This time is correct for all points on the Greenwich meridian, but when you are to the east the passage will be earlier and when to the west, later. The degrees of your DR longitude must be multiplied by four to get minutes (of time), which must then be added to or subtracted from the time of the meridian passage at Greenwich to give you the UT of the meridian passage on your longitude.

For example, on 7 December 1990 (Appendix A) the meridian passage of the Sun is at 11h 51 m. Now at W10° the passage will be (10 x 4) 40 minutes later, at 12h 31m UT. At E10° the passage will be 40m earlier, at 11h 11m.

The theory of this type of sight was explained on page 13; let us now look at two examples of its working, both from Sun sights on 15 July 1990 (Appendix B):

DR Lat. N	54°32′	DR Lat. S	11°10′	
Long.	0°00′	Long. W	30°00′	(2 hours)
	90°00′.0		90°00′.0	
Obs. Alt.	− 57°05′.6		− 57°05′.6	
ZD	32°54′.4		32°54′.4	
Dec. N.	+ 21°31′.4		− 21°30′.6	
LAT	N 54°25′.8		S 11°23′.8	

The Sun appears to remain at the highest point of its trajectory for some time. In our latitudes this varies from about ten minutes in midwinter to four in summer. When it appears on your sextant to have stopped rising, take a series of five sights spread over the next two or three minutes and average them to give your sextant altitude. There is no need to time these sights.

Declination must be taken out for the time of the observation, so that if you are far east or west of the Greenwich meridian the appropriate declination will not be that at 12h UT. In the example above you will see that there are two figures for declination, only slightly different in this case, marking the fact that the second sight is taken in W30°, where noon is two hours later than at Greenwich.

Meridian sights can be taken for any heavenly body, and the local times of the meridian passages of the Moon and the planets are given in the *Nautical Almanac* at the foot of the page. The meridian passages of stars are discussed on page 45.

Meridian sights have three advantages: accurate time is not necessary, the working out is very simple, and there is no plotting on the chart.

Star Sights

SIDEREAL HOUR ANGLE

The GHAs of individual stars are not given in the Almanac. A reference point in the heavens, called the First Point of Aries, has been chosen and its GHA is tabulated in the Almanac as if it were a heavenly body. The stars, for navigational purposes, are fixed in relation to each other and to *Aries,* so that the angle at the Pole between the meridian of *Aries* and the meridian of a particular

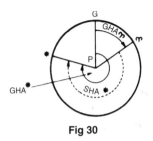

Fig 30

star does not change. This angle, measured in a westerly direction from the meridian of *Aries*, is called Sidereal Hour Angle (SHA). The SHA and declination of 57 selected stars are listed in the *Nautical Almanac* every three days. In Fig 30 we see:

GHA *Aries*: The hour angle of the meridian of *Aries* measured westwards from the Greenwich meridian.

SHA Star: The hour angle of the star measured westwards from the meridian of *Aries*. This angle does not alter.

GHA Star: The hour angle of the star measured westwards from the Greenwich meridian.

This last angle *always* equals the sum of the other two hour angles:

GHA *Aries* + SHA Star = GHA Star

Let us look at an example. On 8 December 1990, DR position N35°43′, E19°12′, *Sirius* is observed at 04h 56m 32s:

GHA *Aries* (04h)	136°39′.4
Increment (56m 32s)	14°10′.3
GHA *Aries*	150°49′.7
SHA *Sirius*	258°48′.2
	409°37′.9
	− 360°
GHA *Sirius*	49°37′.9

Dealing with hour angles, when an addition comes to more than 360°, that figure is subtracted. (Likewise if a minus quantity appears, 360° are added.) The increment to be added to GHA

Aries for the minutes and seconds of GMT is found in the *Aries* column on the "Increments and Corrections" page. Having found GHA Star, LHA Star is obtained in the normal way by adding or subtracting longitude.

DECLINATIONS

The declinations of stars virtually do not change during the year. They are printed, together with SHA, in the Star column in the main body of the Almanac. Provided the declination of a star is less than 30° (north or south) the sight can be worked out from Vols 2 and 3 of H.O. 249 as for other heavenly bodies. H.O. 229 or one of the "short" tables (see page 51) can be used for declinations of more than 30°. H.O. 249 Vol 1 is designed specifically for star sights, however, and is more convenient because it tells you which star to use when, and where it is.

TWILIGHT AND PREPARATION OF STAR SIGHTS

Star sights must be planned to efficiently use the relatively short interval when both stars and the horizon are visible. On the right-hand pages of the *Nautical Almanac*, times are given for the beginning (morning) and end (evening) of nautical and civil twilight, as well as the rising and setting times of the Sun and Moon. The figures in these tables are strictly correct only on the meridian of Greenwich, at the latitudes listed, and on the middle day of the page. However, for planning purposes we need only select the nearest tabulated latitude, and adjust for the nearest degree to DR longitude (4 minutes per degree). The times listed in the Civil Twilight columns are approximately the middle of the good observing interval.

Let us consider an example of planning. The relevant pages of the *Nautical Almanac* are reproduced as Appendix H.

Evening, 12 October 1993; DR position N 33° 25′, W 49° 06′

Civil Twilight ends	
at Greenwich Meridian:	17h 56m UT
Longitude 49° X 4m:	3h 16m
Civil Twilight ends at W 49° :	21h 12m UT

GHA *Aries* 21h:	336° 26.6′
Increment 12m:	03° 00.5′
GHA *Aries* 21h 12m:	339° 27′
Longitude (E add):	49° 06′
LHA *Aries* 21h 12m:	290° 21′

Appropriate stars for observation can now be selected. This can be done with a star chart or with a Star Finder such as the 2102-D (formerly published by the U.S. Government but now available commercially). Thirty of the 57 navigational stars can be used with H.O. 249 Vol.II or Vol.III; these are shown on the "EQUATORIAL STARS" chart in the *Nautical Almanac*. However, the easiest way to select stars is to use H.O. 249 Vol.I (Appendix I).

H.O. 249 Vol.I suggests seven stars for each degree of latitude (N or S) and each degree of LHA *Aries*. The names of the brightest (first magnitude) stars are capitalized, and the names of the three stars best distributed in azimuth for a three-star fix are identified by diamonds. Hc and Zn are given directly; no interpolation for declination or conversion from Z to Zn are necessary.

Let us continue with the example started above:

Latitude N 33°; LHA *Aries* 290° (to the nearest degree)

Turning to the page of H.O. 249 Vol.I for N 33° and going to the line for LHA *Aries* 290°, we find that the three recommended stars are Alpheratz, ANTARES and Alkaid.

Shortly after sunset, we go on deck and prepare to make our observations. We achieve and record the following sights:

	Alpheratz	ANTARES	Alkaid
UT	21:07:40	21:10:44	21:16:11
Ho	28° 43′	17° 54′	28° 03′

In the time remaining before the horizon becomes invisible, we can observe some more stars, or a planet that might be available. Although two stars are enough to give a fix, it is usual to observe at least three. Now we can work the sights (see table below) and plot the fix.

Fig 31 is the plot of these sights. It would be extraordinary luck if all three lines met at a single point; normally they form a small triangular figure often called a "cocked hat." The fix is considered to be at the center of the triangle.

	Alpheratz	ANTARES	Alkaid
UT	21:07:40	21:10:44	21:16:11
GHA *Aries*	336° 26.6′	336° 26.6′	336° 26.6′
Increment	01° 55.4′	02° 41.4′	04° 03.4′
GHA *Aries*	338° 22.0′	339° 08.0′	340° 30.0′
AP Long (E+)	-049° 22.0′	-049° 08.0′	-049° 30.0′
LHA *Aries*	289°	290°	291°
Hc	28° 35′	18° 01′	27° 57′
Ho	28° 43′	17° 54′	28° 03′
Intercept	08 TOWARDS	07 AWAY	06 TOWARDS
Zn	072°	220°	313°

When we have used H.O. 249 Vol. I, we often have to make a final adjustment of the fix obtained as above. Vol. I applies exactly only for the year ("Epoch") for which it was calculated. Table 5, Correction for Precession and Nutation, at the back of Vol. I, tells us how to adjust the fix for any year within 4 years (either way) of the Epoch year. The inputs to this table are the year,

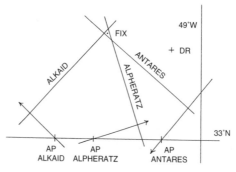

Fig 31

44

the approximate latitude, and the approximate LHA of *Aries*. The outputs are the distance and direction the fix should be moved. For the example above, using Vol.I Epoch 1995.0 in 1993, at a latitude of N 33° and with LHA *Aries* approximately 300°, the adjustment is zero, but if LHA *Aries* had been nearer to 330° than to 300° the adjustment would have been 1 mile in direction 240°. (Precession and nutation are two slow changes of the direction of the Earth's axis in space.) This correction applies *only* to position lines or fixes obtained via H.O. 249 Vol. I.

USING THE MERIDIAN PASSAGE

Each star crosses the observer's meridian when LHA *Aries* = 360°– SHA Star. To find the time of a given LHA *Aries* the observer's longitude must be added (W) or subtracted from (E) LHA to get GHA; the time (UT) of this GHA is then found in the Almanac. For example, to find the time of the meridian passage of *Sirius* in Long W10° on 7 December 1990:

SHA *Sirius* 258°48′.2

360° – 258°48′.2	= 101°11′.8 = LHA *Aries*
101°11′8 + 10° (Long W)	= 111°11′.8 = GHA *Aries*
GHA *Aries* at 02h	= 105°35′.4
diff	5°36′.4

By inspecting the Almanac, we find that at 02h GHA *Aries* is 105°35′.4 and that 5°36′.4 is the increment for 22m 22s, giving a meridian passage of *Sirius* at 02h 22m 22s UT.

Pole Star Sights

As has already been said, if *Polaris* were directly over the North Pole (declination N 90°), its observed altitude would be the latitude of the observer. However, the declination of Polaris is (in 1990) about N 89° 13.5′ (i.e., its GP is nearly 47 miles from the pole), so a correction is necessary.

When you take your sight of *Polaris*, notice the time—the nearest minute will do. Let us say that your sight was at about 03h 15m UT on 15 July 1990; DR N52°50′, E03°42′. The sextant altitude (preferably three averaged readings) is corrected as for a star or planet (index error and dip followed by refraction from the Altitude Correction Tables—Appendix D) to give true altitude.

From the Almanac now find the appropriate GHA *Aries* and correct it for longitude to arrive at LHA *Aries*. Turning to the *Polaris* tables in the *Nautical Almanac* three corrections tables (a_0, a_1, a_2) are found on the same page and are entered with arguments LHA, latitude and month. The three corrections, all taken from the same column determined by LHA, are then added, always, to observed altitude and 1° subtracted to arrive at Latitude. It takes longer to describe than to work:

GHA *Aries* (03h)	337°42′.7	Obs. Alt.		53°14′.0
Increment (15m)	3°45′.6	a_0 (345°10′)	+	29′.4
DR Long. E	3°42′.0 (E+)	a_1 (Lat.53)	+	.6
LHA *Aries*	345°10′.3	a_2 (July)	+	.3
		−1°		−1° 00′.0
		LAT		52°44′.3

Notes

Sextants

A sextant is so called because the arc at the bottom is one-sixth of a circle (60°). However, it measures 120° because moving the index arm 1° moves the image of the Sun by 2°. The attractive, but seldom seen, octant is based on one-eighth of a circle and measures 90°. Smaller and easier to stow than a sextant, it is quite adequate for normal navigational purposes. The principles of a sextant and an octant are the same and we can call them all sextants for convenience.

When you look through the eyepiece of your sextant you see part of a rectangular frame. The left-hand side is plain glass through which you can see the horizon, the right-hand side of this is a mirror that reflects the light from another mirror that is fixed to the top of the sextant and swings with the index arm. The bottom of the index arm swings along a scale calibrated in degrees. The minutes of arc are read off the wheel by which the small adjustments are made. In older sextants, minutes are (with difficulty) read off the degree scale with the help of a vernier.

Cover the top mirror with one or two of the tinted shades, then face the Sun and look through the eyepiece at the horizon (or the garden fence) underneath the Sun. Move the index arm very slowly until the Sun appears, then with the small adjuster wheel "move" the Sun until it rests on the horizon. This is your sight. Read your sextant to the nearest half minute: the result is your sextant altitude.

Sextants are delicate instruments and must be treated carefully. Various errors can occur of which the chief are listed below.

Instrument Error   This is the basic error of the sextant scale. It is determined by the manufacturer for each individual instrument, by comparing the completed instrument to a high-precision standard. It is usually marked on a slip of paper glued to the inside of the lid of the box. It is usually very small.

Index Error   This is simply an offset of the sextant scale from where it should be. It is rarely zero, because the adjustment to reduce index error interacts with the very important adjustments that ensure that the sextant mirrors are perpendicular to the plane of the scale. If you try to totally eliminate index error, you will waste time and cause needless wear of the adjusting screws. An index error of 5′, or even more, is quite acceptable as long as you know what it is. You should check it frequently; a sudden change is an indication that the instrument may have been abused and may no longer be trustworthy.

To check index error, set the sextant roughly at zero and look at the Sun (do not forget the shades). You will see two suns: bring them so that their edges are just touching and read the sextant, then reverse the suns and read it again. You will find that one reading will be the ordinary scale (on) and one on the minus side (off). Subtract the smaller from the larger, halve it, and the result is the index error, to be added when the greater number is "off," and subtracted when "on." You can test the accuracy of your reading by adding the two figures: the sum should equal four times the semi-diameter of the Sun. The sum might look like this:

17 July 1990, SD 15′8 (from bottom of Sun column in Almanac)

	Sextant readings		check	
	33′.2 on			33′.2
	30′.0 off			30′.0
	2)3′.2		4)63′.2	
Index error	1′.6 on			15′.8

Taken to the nearest half minute, the index error is 1′.5 "on," and this must be subtracted from the sextant altitude.

There is another, less accurate but quicker, way of checking the index error on a really clear day. Set your sextant at zero and you will see two horizons. Turn the wheel until these form one straight line when the reading should, but will probably not, be zero: the difference is the index error.

Calculators

Specialized navigational calculators or calculators with navigational software take what little hard work there is left out of celestial. However, before you rush off to buy one, try out a friend's to make sure that it is really worthwhile adding such an expensive item to your equipment. Remember that you will never be able to dispense entirely with your almanac and tables because all batteries can run down and electronic gear is not a lover of salt water.

Let us look at what a calculator can do. Sextants exist that average sight and time as you take the sights, but failing one of those you must take the sights and time them. The previously tiresome and error-prone averaging is a few seconds' work for programs that use minutes and seconds of arc as easily as decimals.

The calculator's main function is to resolve the spherical triangle that, we have seen, lies behind every sight. The old Cosine-Haversine method of working out sights used the ship's DR for the assumed position (Z in Fig 19). The disadvantage of precalculated sight reduction tables such as H.O. 249 and H.O. 229 is that the assumed position must be chosen to suit the tables (i.e., latitude and LHA must be integral degrees). This sometimes makes plotting awkward. Using a calculator, the DR position can, once again, be the starting point for our chartwork.

There are many other navigational uses to which calculators can be put. Apart from practical use, a calculator with trigonometric functions makes for easy understanding of navigational problems. The *Nautical Almanac* includes a section entitled "Sight Reduction Procedures: Methods and Formulae for Direct Computation," which gives a number of examples which should be studied. Those with a little mathematical ability may find that they can resolve the following equations without too much difficulty.

(i)   sin Alt = sin Lat sin Dec + cos Lat cos Dec cos LHA

In this formula, which supplies the calculated altitude, as in others, declination may be positive or negative; when *same* name as Lat (both S or both N) it is positive, when *opposite* name negative. (The "Cosine-Haversine" method referred to above is a modification of this formula that is somewhat less liable to human error when using logarithms.)

(ii) $$\cos \text{ azimuth angle} = \frac{\sin \text{Dec} - \sin \text{Alt} \sin \text{Lat}}{\cos \text{Alt} \cos \text{Lat}}$$

Formulas (i) and (ii) are the ones from which H.O. 249 and H.O. 229 were calculated.

(iii)   cos great circle distance =
sin Lat1 sin Lat2 + cos Lat1 cos Lat2 cos diff Long

Above, 1 and 2 refer to the starting point and destination.

Formula (iii) is identical with formula (i) and gives you the distance between, say, Bermuda and the Bishop Rock Light. The answer will appear as degrees and minutes, so the degrees must be multiplied by 60 to reduce them to nautical miles.

How much longer would the rhumb line distance be than that of the great circle? The rhumb line distance is given by:

(iv) $$\frac{60 \text{ diff Lat}}{\cos \text{ rhumb line course}}$$

It may appear as a minus figure, but ignore the sign.

If you want to know the declination of a rising or setting body, then:

(v)   sin Dec = cos Lat cos azimuth

but be aware that the formula does not take account of dip or refraction.

The rhumb line course, which may not be easy to measure from the chart, is given by:

(vi) $$\tan C = \frac{\pi \text{ (diff Long)}}{180[\ln \tan (45 + \text{Lat2}/2) - \ln \tan (45 + \text{Lat1}/2)]}$$

where C is the rhumb line course. This formula looks awful, but starting at the bottom right and working backwards it is really quite easy. The calculator will give you an angle between −90° and +90°. If you get a negative angle, add 180° to it. You now have an angle between zero and 180°. If the destination lies east of the origin, this angle is the (true) course; if the destination lies west, subtract this angle from 360° to get the course.

The azimuth of any body at its rising or setting (when ZD = 90°) permits you to check your compass and can be found by:

(vii)
$$\cos \text{azimuth} = \frac{\sin \text{Dec}}{\cos \text{Lat}}$$

The ratio "Long per inch:Lat per inch" on a Mercator chart is given by

(viii)
$$\text{Long:Lat} = \cos \text{Lat}$$

At the push of a button or two, a specialized navigational calculator offers an almanac for several decades for at least the Sun and *Aries*, the various answers to all the formulae above, altitude corrections, noon sights, course and speed made good, workings in arc or time, and a host of other possibilities. My NC77 adds, unsurprisingly, to the speed and accuracy of any work, but I find it also adds amazingly to my interest in the subject—perhaps because, among other reasons, it removes the constant nagging doubt as to whether I have done the last addition correctly.

"Short" Sight Reduction Tables

There are several very compact alternatives to the quite bulky precalculated sight reduction tables like H.O. 249 and H.O. 229. These are often referred to generically as "short" tables, and indeed they are short, but they are rather more tedious to use than the precalculated tables. The most common of the short tables are:

1   "Concise Sight Reduction Tables" devised recently by Rear Admiral Thomas D. Davies, USN. Initially published commercially (Cornell Maritime Press, 1984), these are now incorporated into the *Nautical Almanac*, making the

Almanac the only book you absolutely must have. The tables occupy 32 pages.

2 H.O. 211, devised in 1931 by then Lieut. (later Rear Admiral) Arthur A. Ageton, USN. In various forms, this has been the longest lived of all the short tables, although it is no longer in print as a separate Government publication. The tables are reprinted in Volume II of the 1975 edition of H.O. 9, "The American Practical Navigator," and have also been reprinted commercially. The tables occupy 36 pages.

3 "Compact Sight Reduction Table", by Allan E. Bayless (Cornell Maritime Press, 1980, 1989). This is a condensed and refined version of H.O. 211. The tables occupy only 9 pages.

4 "Celestial Navigation With The S TABLE", by Mike Pepperday (Paradise Cay Publications, 1992). This is also based on the method of H.O. 211, and the tables occupy 9 pages. The instructions include a procedure for using the same worksheet with a scientific calculator instead of the tables.

The "Concise Tables" put the same limitations on choice of assumed position as do the precalculated tables (i.e. latitude and LHA must be integral degrees). The tables based on H.O. 211 can use the DR position as the assumed position.

The accuracy of any of these short tables is entirely adequate for yacht navigation, but their procedures are more liable to human error. For example, I find that in using the "Concise Tables" I must take care to get the right sign (+ or –), and one must remember that A, F and P are taken to the *nearest* degree, unlike most other tables where the *next lower* degree is taken. But those who practice will soon learn, and the convenience is undeniable.

Here is our Sun sight of 7 December worked with the "Concise Tables":

Lat 52°   LHA 348°   Dec – 22° 36′
Reduction table, 1st entry

	(Lat, LHA)=(52,348)	A=	7°21	A°= 7,	A′= 21
		B=	+ 37 23		Z_1= + 80.5
		Dec=	– 22 36		
		F=	14 47	F°=15,	F′= 47

Reduction table, 2nd entry
(A°, F°) = (7,15)   H= 14°53′ P°=83, Z_2 = + 88.1

Aux table, 1st entry
(F′, P°) = (47, 83)   −   13

                          14 40 Z_1 = + 80.5
Aux table, 2nd entry   −   1 Z_2 = + 88.1
(A′, Z_2) = (21, 88)   Hc 14°39′   Z = 168.6=Zn

This calculated altitude 14°39′ is to be compared with that using H.O. 249, which was 14°40′. The azimuths are 168.6° and 169° so in these sights there is little to choose between the systems.

Practice Sights

Useful experience can be gained at home finding the whereabouts of your house with an artificial horizon. This is a horizontal reflecting surface that enables you to measure with your sextant the angle between the heavenly body and its reflection; the angle is double the altitude of the Sun.

The simplest form of artificial horizon is water in a bucket, but unless it is covered with oil it can only be used in very calm weather or the ripples distort the reflection. Ideally, a shallow bowl of mercury or oil is used, which gives a better and steadier reflection.

On a windless sunny day, place yourself in line with the Sun and the bucket and with the sextant bring the "real" Sun down to its reflection. Superimpose the two suns and take a series of five sights, about one a minute, timing them carefully. Average these observations and then halve the resulting angle to obtain sextant altitude. Corrections for dip and semi-diameter are not needed, but those for index error and refraction must be applied to arrive at observed altitude. The Altitude Correction Table for Stars and Planets (Appendix D) is to be used for refraction.

A sight of the Moon is easy to take and is less dazzling than the Sun. Use the instructions given in the Moon Altitude Correction Tables (Appendix E) for bubble sextants for correcting the sextant altitude.

If your position line does not pass directly through your

house you may have made a mistake in the sight or you may not know where you live and have placed your house incorrectly on the plotting sheet.

Plotting Sheets

There are occasions when the chart is not suitable for plotting observations. Practicing on land, the chart may not cover your area; far out to sea, the chart may not be of a scale to permit accurate plotting of a series of sights, or even if it is, the resulting mass of lines might make it almost unusable. It is easy to make a plotting sheet, which shows only latitude and longitude, at any scale you like (say 5 millimeters per nautical mile) and for any latitude. You will need to know the Long:Lat ratio at your chosen latitude. The ratio can be found geometrically or mathematically (by formula viii on page 51).

Fig 32 shows how to find this ratio geometrically. Angle A is drawn the size of the required latitude (here, 50°). Mark 1 to 10 miles (same as minutes of latitude), at the desired scale, along

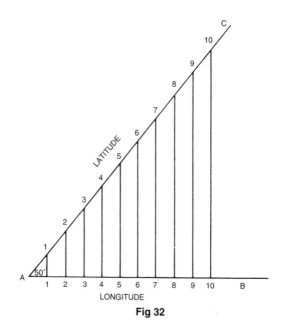

Fig 32

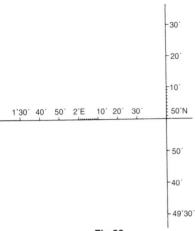

Fig 33

AC and drop perpendiculars to AB. AB is now the scale of 1 to 10 minutes of longitude at the chosen latitude. Actually, you often need not construct a complete scale; you usually only need to convert the few longitudes of your assumed positions, perhaps reversing the process to convert the longitude of your plotted fix to a numerical longitude. Great accuracy is required: an error of 1° in low latitudes will cause little distortion, but any inaccuracy in high latitudes will be directly reflected in the plotted position.

Using a calculator or tables, simply multiply the number of minutes of longitude by cos Lat to get the number of miles and plot at the desired scale. For example, to locate the assumed position for the Sun line in Fig 28 (W 20° 16.5′ on N 40°, at a scale of 10 mm per nm), multiply

$$16.5 \times \cos 40° \times 10 = 16.5 \times 0.766 \times 10 = 12.6 \text{ mm}$$

and plot this distance westward from the line representing W 20°.

The U.S. Government publishes a Universal Plotting Sheet (called VP-OS), sold in pads of 50, which has a compass rose, one meridian and three parallels of latitude pre-printed. This simplifies plotting longitudes at any desired latitude.

It is also possible to construct a plotting sheet with a given scale per degree of longitude, using the inverse ratio 1/cos Lat.

Fig 33 shows a home-made plotting sheet for use at latitude 50° N and any required longitude (here shown between 1°30′ and 2°30′E). The continuous change in the Long:Lat ratio from the equator to the poles makes it inadvisable for a home-made sheet to cover more than 2° of latitude. This will always be adequate if the latitude of your assumed position has been correctly chosen.

Appendix A

1990 DECEMBER 6, 7, 8 (THURS., FRI., SAT.)

UT (GMT)	SUN G.H.A.	Dec.	MOON G.H.A.	v	Dec.	d	H.P.
d h	° ′	° ′	° ′	′	° ′	′	′
6 00	182 18.7	S22 26.1	307 31.5	7.7	N18 33.4	11.8	59.6
01	197 18.4	26.4	321 58.2	8.0	18 21.6	11.8	59.6
02	212 18.1	26.7	336 25.2	8.0	18 09.8	11.9	59.5
03	227 17.9	.. 27.0	350 52.2	8.1	17 57.9	11.9	59.5
04	242 17.6	27.3	5 19.3	8.3	17 46.0	12.1	59.5
05	257 17.4	27.6	19 46.6	8.4	17 33.9	12.2	59.4
T 06	272 17.1	S22 27.9	34 14.0	8.6	N17 21.7	12.2	59.4
H 07	287 16.8	28.2	48 41.6	8.7	17 09.5	12.4	59.3
U 08	302 16.6	28.5	63 09.3	8.7	16 57.1	12.4	59.3
R 09	317 16.3	.. 28.8	77 37.0	9.0	16 44.7	12.5	59.3
S 10	332 16.0	29.1	92 05.0	9.0	16 32.2	12.5	59.2
D 11	347 15.8	29.4	106 33.0	9.2	16 19.7	12.7	59.2
A 12	2 15.5	S22 29.7	121 01.2	9.2	N16 07.0	12.7	59.1
Y 13	17 15.3	30.0	135 29.4	9.4	15 54.3	12.8	59.1
14	32 15.0	30.3	149 57.8	9.6	15 41.5	12.8	59.1
15	47 14.7	.. 30.6	164 26.4	9.6	15 28.7	12.9	59.0
16	62 14.5	30.9	178 55.0	9.7	15 15.8	13.0	59.0
17	77 14.2	31.2	193 23.7	9.9	15 02.8	13.1	58.9
18	92 13.9	S22 31.5	207 52.6	10.0	N14 49.7	13.1	58.9
19	107 13.7	31.8	222 21.6	10.1	14 36.6	13.2	58.9
20	122 13.4	32.1	236 50.7	10.2	14 23.4	13.2	58.8
21	137 13.1	.. 32.4	251 19.9	10.4	14 10.2	13.3	58.8
22	152 12.9	32.7	265 49.3	10.4	13 56.9	13.4	58.7
23	167 12.6	33.0	280 18.7	10.5	13 43.5	13.4	58.7
7 00	182 12.3	S22 33.2	294 48.2	10.7	N13 30.1	13.4	58.7
01	197 12.1	33.5	309 17.9	10.8	13 16.7	13.5	58.6
02	212 11.8	33.8	323 47.7	10.8	13 03.2	13.6	58.6
03	227 11.5	.. 34.1	338 17.5	11.0	12 49.6	13.6	58.5
04	242 11.3	34.4	352 47.5	11.1	12 36.0	13.6	58.5
05	257 11.0	34.7	7 17.6	11.2	12 22.4	13.7	58.5
F 06	272 10.7	S22 35.0	21 47.8	11.2	N12 08.7	13.8	58.4
R 07	287 10.5	35.3	36 18.0	11.4	11 54.9	13.7	58.4
I 08	302 10.2	35.5	50 48.4	11.5	11 41.2	13.8	58.3
D 09	317 09.9	.. 35.8	65 18.9	11.6	11 27.4	13.9	58.3
A 10	332 09.7	36.1	79 49.5	11.7	11 13.5	13.9	58.3
Y 11	347 09.4	36.4	94 20.2	11.7	10 59.6	13.9	58.2
12	2 09.1	S22 36.7	108 50.9	11.9	N10 45.7	14.0	58.2
13	17 08.9	36.9	123 21.8	12.0	10 31.7	14.0	58.1
14	32 08.6	37.2	137 52.8	12.0	10 17.7	14.0	58.1
15	47 08.3	.. 37.5	152 23.8	12.1	10 03.7	14.0	58.1
16	62 08.1	37.8	166 54.9	12.3	9 49.7	14.1	58.0
17	77 07.8	38.1	181 26.2	12.3	9 35.6	14.1	58.0
18	92 07.5	S22 38.3	195 57.5	12.4	N 9 21.5	14.2	57.9
19	107 07.3	38.6	210 28.9	12.5	9 07.3	14.1	57.9
20	122 07.0	38.9	225 00.4	12.5	8 53.2	14.2	57.9
21	137 06.7	.. 39.2	239 31.9	12.7	8 39.0	14.2	57.8
22	152 06.4	39.4	254 03.6	12.7	8 24.8	14.2	57.8
23	167 06.2	39.7	268 35.3	12.8	8 10.6	14.3	57.8
8 00	182 05.9	S22 40.0	283 07.1	12.9	N 7 56.3	14.2	57.7
01	197 05.6	40.3	297 39.0	13.0	7 42.1	14.3	57.7
02	212 05.4	40.5	312 11.0	13.0	7 27.8	14.3	57.6
03	227 05.1	.. 40.8	326 43.0	13.1	7 13.5	14.3	57.6
04	242 04.8	41.1	341 15.1	13.2	6 59.2	14.3	57.5
05	257 04.5	41.3	355 47.3	13.3	6 44.9	14.3	57.5
S 06	272 04.3	S22 41.6	10 19.6	13.3	N 6 30.6	14.4	57.5
A 07	287 04.0	41.9	24 51.9	13.4	6 16.2	14.3	57.4
T 08	302 03.7	42.1	39 24.3	13.5	6 01.9	14.4	57.4
U 09	317 03.5	.. 42.4	53 56.8	13.5	5 47.5	14.3	57.4
R 10	332 03.2	42.7	68 29.3	13.6	5 33.2	14.4	57.3
D 11	347 02.9	42.9	83 01.9	13.7	5 18.8	14.4	57.3
A 12	2 02.6	S22 43.2	97 34.6	13.7	N 5 04.4	14.3	57.3
Y 13	17 02.4	43.5	112 07.3	13.8	4 50.1	14.4	57.2
14	32 02.1	43.7	126 40.1	13.8	4 35.7	14.4	57.2
15	47 01.8	.. 44.0	141 12.9	13.9	4 21.3	14.4	57.1
16	62 01.5	44.2	155 45.8	14.0	4 06.9	14.3	57.1
17	77 01.3	44.5	170 18.8	14.0	3 52.6	14.4	57.1
18	92 01.0	S22 44.7	184 51.8	14.0	N 3 38.2	14.4	57.0
19	107 00.7	45.0	199 24.8	14.1	3 23.8	14.4	57.0
20	122 00.4	45.3	213 57.9	14.2	3 09.4	14.3	57.0
21	137 00.2	.. 45.5	228 31.1	14.2	2 55.1	14.4	56.9
22	151 59.9	45.8	243 04.3	14.3	2 40.7	14.3	56.9
23	166 59.6	46.0	257 37.6	14.3	2 26.4	14.4	56.9
	S.D. 16.3	d 0.3	S.D. 16.1		15.9		15.6

Moonrise

Lat.	Twilight Naut.	Civil	Sunrise	6	7	8	9
°	h m	h m	h m	h m	h m	h m	h m
N 72	08 05	10 16	■	18 38	21 13	23 23	25 24
N 70	07 47	09 29	■	19 11	21 27	23 26	25 19
68	07 33	08 58	11 17	19 35	21 38	23 29	25 14
66	07 21	08 35	10 06	19 53	21 47	23 31	25 10
64	07 11	08 17	09 31	20 08	21 54	23 33	25 07
62	07 02	08 02	09 05	20 20	22 00	23 34	25 04
60	06 54	07 50	08 46	20 30	22 06	23 36	25 02
N 58	06 47	07 39	08 29	20 39	22 11	23 37	25 00
56	06 41	07 29	08 16	20 47	22 15	23 38	24 58
54	06 35	07 21	08 04	20 54	22 19	23 39	24 56
52	06 30	07 13	07 53	21 00	22 22	23 40	24 54
50	06 25	07 06	07 44	21 06	22 25	23 41	24 53
45	06 14	06 51	07 24	21 18	22 32	23 42	24 50
N 40	06 04	06 38	07 08	21 28	22 38	23 44	24 47
35	05 55	06 26	06 54	21 36	22 42	23 45	24 45
30	05 47	06 16	06 43	21 44	22 47	23 46	24 43
20	05 31	05 58	06 22	21 56	22 54	23 48	24 40
N 10	05 16	05 42	06 04	22 08	23 00	23 50	24 37
0	04 59	05 25	05 48	22 18	23 06	23 52	24 35
S 10	04 41	05 08	05 31	22 28	23 12	23 53	24 32
20	04 19	04 48	05 13	22 39	23 19	23 55	24 29
30	03 51	04 24	04 51	22 52	23 26	23 57	24 26
35	03 33	04 10	04 39	22 59	23 30	23 58	24 25
40	03 11	03 52	04 25	23 07	23 35	23 59	24 23
45	02 42	03 31	04 07	23 16	23 40	24 01	00 01
S 50	02 00	03 03	03 46	23 28	23 46	24 03	00 03
52	01 36	02 48	03 36	23 33	23 49	24 03	00 03
54	01 00	02 32	03 24	23 39	23 53	24 04	00 04
56	////	02 11	03 11	23 45	23 56	24 05	00 05
58	////	01 45	02 55	23 52	24 00	00 00	00 06
S 60	////	01 07	02 36	24 00	00 00	00 05	00 08

Moonset

Lat.	Twilight Sunset	Civil	Naut.	6	7	8	9
°	h m	h m	h m	h m	h m	h m	h m
N 72	■	13 26	15 37	13 56	13 04	12 31	12 03
N 70	■	14 14	15 55	13 21	12 48	12 24	12 04
68	12 26	14 44	16 09	13 35	12 35	12 19	12 05
66	13 36	15 07	16 21	12 35	12 24	12 14	12 05
64	14 12	15 25	16 32	12 19	12 15	12 10	12 06
62	14 37	15 40	16 41	12 05	12 07	12 07	12 06
60	14 57	15 53	16 48	11 55	12 00	12 04	12 07
N 58	15 13	16 04	16 55	11 45	11 54	12 01	12 07
56	15 27	16 13	17 02	11 36	11 49	11 59	12 08
54	15 39	16 22	17 08	11 28	11 44	11 57	12 08
52	15 49	16 30	17 13	11 21	11 40	11 55	12 08
50	15 59	16 37	17 18	11 15	11 36	11 53	12 09
45	16 18	16 54	17 30	11 01	11 27	11 49	12 09
N 40	16 35	17 05	17 39	10 50	11 20	11 46	12 10
35	16 48	17 16	17 48	10 40	11 14	11 43	12 10
30	17 00	17 26	17 56	10 31	11 08	11 40	12 11
20	17 20	17 44	18 12	10 16	10 58	11 36	12 12
N 10	17 38	18 01	18 27	10 03	10 50	11 32	12 12
0	17 55	18 18	18 44	09 51	10 41	11 28	12 12
S 10	18 12	18 35	19 02	09 38	10 33	11 24	12 13
20	18 30	18 55	19 24	09 25	10 24	11 20	12 13
30	18 52	19 19	19 52	09 09	10 14	11 16	12 14
35	19 04	19 33	20 10	09 00	10 08	11 13	12 14
40	19 19	19 51	20 32	08 50	10 02	11 10	12 15
45	19 37	20 13	21 01	08 37	09 54	11 06	12 15
S 50	19 57	20 41	21 44	08 22	09 44	11 02	12 16
52	20 08	20 55	22 08	08 15	09 40	11 00	12 16
54	20 19	21 12	22 45	08 07	09 35	10 57	12 16
56	20 33	21 32	////	07 58	09 29	10 55	12 16
58	20 48	21 59	////	07 48	09 23	10 52	12 17
S 60	21 07	22 39	////	07 37	09 16	10 49	12 17

SUN / MOON

Day	SUN Eqn. of Time 00h	12h	Mer. Pass.	MOON Mer. Pass. Upper	Lower	Age	Phase
	m s	m s	h m	h m	h m		
6	09 15	09 03	11 51	03 38	16 04	19	☽
7	08 50	08 37	11 51	04 30	16 54	20	
8	08 24	08 11	11 52	05 17	17 40	21	

Appendix B

1990 JULY 15, 16, 17 (SUN., MON., TUES.)

SUN and MOON

UT (GMT)	SUN G.H.A.	Dec.	MOON G.H.A.	v	Dec.	d	H.P.
15 00	178 32.1	N21 36.1	279 31.2	11.4	N10 55.9	14.6	58.7
01	193 32.0	35.7	294 01.6	11.3	11 10.5	14.4	58.7
02	208 31.9	35.3	308 31.9	11.2	11 24.9	14.4	58.7
03	223 31.9	.. 34.9	323 02.1	11.1	11 39.3	14.4	58.7
04	238 31.8	34.5	337 32.2	11.1	11 53.7	14.3	58.7
05	253 31.7	34.2	352 02.3	11.0	12 08.0	14.3	58.8
06	268 31.7	N21 33.8	6 32.3	10.9	N12 22.3	14.2	58.8
07	283 31.6	33.4	21 02.2	10.8	12 36.5	14.1	58.8
S 08	298 31.5	33.0	35 32.0	10.7	12 50.6	14.1	58.8
U 09	313 31.5	.. 32.6	50 01.7	10.6	13 04.7	14.0	58.9
N 10	328 31.4	32.2	64 31.3	10.6	13 18.7	14.0	58.9
D 11	343 31.3	31.8	79 00.9	10.4	13 32.7	13.9	58.9
A 12	358 31.3	N21 31.4	93 30.3	10.4	N13 46.6	13.9	58.9
Y 13	13 31.2	31.0	107 59.7	10.3	14 00.5	13.8	58.9
14	28 31.2	30.6	122 29.0	10.2	14 14.3	13.7	59.0
15	43 31.1	.. 30.2	136 58.2	10.1	14 28.0	13.6	59.0
16	58 31.0	29.8	151 27.3	10.0	14 41.6	13.6	59.0
17	73 31.0	29.8	165 56.3	9.9	14 55.2	13.5	59.0
18	88 30.9	N21 29.0	180 25.2	9.8	N15 08.7	13.5	59.0
19	103 30.8	28.6	194 54.0	9.7	15 22.2	13.3	59.1
20	118 30.8	28.2	209 22.7	9.7	15 35.5	13.3	59.1
21	133 30.7	.. 27.8	223 51.4	9.5	15 48.8	13.2	59.1
22	148 30.6	27.4	238 19.9	9.4	16 02.0	13.1	59.1
23	163 30.6	27.0	252 48.3	9.3	16 15.1	13.1	59.1
16 00	178 30.5	N21 26.6	267 16.6	9.3	N16 28.2	12.9	59.2
01	193 30.5	26.2	281 44.9	9.1	16 41.1	12.9	59.2
02	208 30.4	25.8	296 13.0	9.0	16 54.0	12.8	59.2
03	223 30.3	.. 25.4	310 41.0	8.9	17 06.8	12.7	59.2
04	238 30.3	25.0	325 08.9	8.8	17 19.5	12.6	59.2
05	253 30.2	24.6	339 36.7	8.7	17 32.1	12.5	59.3
06	268 30.2	N21 24.2	354 04.4	8.7	N17 44.6	12.4	59.3
07	283 30.1	23.8	8 32.1	8.5	17 57.0	12.4	59.3
M 08	298 30.0	23.4	22 59.6	8.4	18 09.4	12.2	59.3
O 09	313 30.0	.. 23.0	37 27.0	8.2	18 21.6	12.1	59.3
N 10	328 29.9	22.6	51 54.2	8.2	18 33.7	12.1	59.4
D 11	343 29.9	22.2	66 21.4	8.1	18 45.8	11.9	59.4
A 12	358 29.8	N21 21.8	80 48.5	8.0	N18 57.7	11.8	59.4
Y 13	13 29.7	21.3	95 15.5	7.8	19 09.5	11.7	59.4
14	28 29.7	20.9	109 42.3	7.8	19 21.2	11.6	59.4
15	43 29.6	.. 20.5	124 09.1	7.6	19 32.8	11.5	59.5
16	58 29.6	20.1	138 35.7	7.6	19 44.3	11.4	59.5
17	73 29.5	19.7	153 02.3	7.4	19 55.7	11.3	59.5
18	88 29.4	N21 19.3	167 28.7	7.3	N20 07.0	11.2	59.5
19	103 29.4	18.9	181 55.0	7.2	20 18.2	11.0	59.5
20	118 29.3	18.5	196 21.2	7.1	20 29.2	10.9	59.6
21	133 29.3	.. 18.0	210 47.3	7.0	20 40.1	10.8	59.6
22	148 29.2	17.6	225 13.3	6.9	20 50.9	10.7	59.6
23	163 29.2	17.2	239 39.2	6.7	21 01.6	10.6	59.6
17 00	178 29.1	N21 16.8	254 04.9	6.7	N21 12.2	10.4	59.6
01	193 29.0	16.4	268 30.6	6.6	21 22.6	10.3	59.6
02	208 29.0	16.0	282 56.2	6.4	21 32.9	10.2	59.6
03	223 28.9	.. 15.5	297 21.6	6.3	21 43.1	10.0	59.7
04	238 28.9	15.1	311 46.9	6.3	21 53.1	9.9	59.7
05	253 28.8	14.7	326 12.2	6.1	22 03.0	9.8	59.7
06	268 28.8	N21 14.3	340 37.3	6.0	N22 12.8	9.6	59.7
07	283 28.7	13.9	355 02.3	5.9	22 22.4	9.5	59.7
T 08	298 28.7	13.4	9 27.2	5.8	22 31.9	9.4	59.7
U 09	313 28.6	.. 13.0	23 52.0	5.7	22 41.3	9.2	59.7
E 10	328 28.5	12.6	38 16.7	5.6	22 50.5	9.0	59.8
S 11	343 28.5	12.2	52 41.3	5.4	22 59.5	9.0	59.8
D 12	358 28.4	N21 11.7	67 05.7	5.4	N23 08.5	8.7	59.8
A 13	13 28.4	11.3	81 30.1	5.3	23 17.2	8.7	59.8
Y 14	28 28.3	10.9	95 54.4	5.2	23 25.9	8.4	59.8
15	43 28.3	.. 10.5	110 18.6	5.0	23 34.3	8.4	59.8
16	58 28.2	10.0	124 42.6	5.0	23 42.7	8.1	59.9
17	73 28.2	09.6	139 06.6	4.9	23 50.8	8.1	59.9
18	88 28.1	N21 09.2	153 30.5	4.7	N23 58.9	7.8	59.9
19	103 28.1	08.8	167 54.2	4.7	24 06.7	7.7	59.9
20	118 28.0	08.3	182 17.9	4.6	24 14.4	7.5	59.9
21	133 28.0	.. 07.9	196 41.5	4.5	24 21.9	7.4	59.9
22	148 27.9	07.5	211 05.0	4.4	24 29.3	7.2	59.9
23	163 27.9	07.0	225 28.4	4.3	24 36.5	7.1	59.9
	S.D. 15.8	d 0.4	S.D. 16.1		16.2		16.3

Twilight, Sunrise and Moonrise

Lat.	Naut.	Civil	Sunrise	Moonrise 15	16	17	18
N 72	□	□	□	20 09	□	□	□
N 70	□	□	□	20 44	□	□	□
68	////	□	□	21 09	20 27	□	□
66	////	////	01 38	21 28	21 08	□	□
64	////	////	02 17	21 44	21 36	21 24	□
62	////	00 54	02 44	21 57	21 58	22 03	22 20
60	////	01 47	03 05	22 09	22 16	22 30	23 00
N 58	□	02 17	03 22	22 19	22 31	22 51	23 28
56	00 50	02 40	03 36	22 27	22 44	23 09	23 50
54	01 38	02 58	03 48	22 35	22 55	23 24	24 08
52	02 06	03 13	03 59	22 42	23 05	23 37	24 23
50	02 28	03 26	04 08	22 48	23 14	23 48	24 37
45	03 06	03 52	04 28	23 02	23 33	24 12	00 12
N 40	03 33	04 12	04 44	23 13	23 48	24 32	00 32
35	03 53	04 29	04 58	23 23	24 02	00 02	00 48
30	04 10	04 43	05 09	23 32	24 13	00 13	01 02
20	04 37	05 05	05 29	23 46	24 33	00 33	01 26
N 10	04 57	05 24	05 46	24 00	00 00	00 50	01 47
0	05 14	05 40	06 02	24 12	00 12	01 07	02 06
S 10	05 30	05 56	06 18	24 24	00 24	01 23	02 26
20	05 44	06 11	06 35	24 38	00 38	01 41	02 47
30	05 59	06 28	06 54	24 53	00 53	02 02	03 12
35	06 06	06 38	07 05	25 02	01 02	02 14	03 27
40	06 15	06 48	07 18	00 00	01 13	02 28	03 43
45	06 23	07 00	07 33	00 08	01 25	02 45	04 04
S 50	06 33	07 14	07 51	00 17	01 40	03 05	04 30
52	06 38	07 20	08 00	00 21	01 47	03 15	04 42
54	06 43	07 28	08 09	00 26	01 55	03 27	04 56
56	06 48	07 35	08 20	00 31	02 04	03 39	05 13
58	06 53	07 44	08 33	00 37	02 14	03 54	05 33
S 60	07 00	07 54	08 47	00 44	02 25	04 12	05 59

Sunset, Twilight and Moonset

Lat.	Sunset	Civil	Naut.	Moonset 15	16	17	18
N 72	□	□	□	15 22	□	□	□
N 70	□	□	□	14 49	□	□	□
68	□	□	□	14 26	16 59	□	□
66	22 30	////	////	14 08	16 19	□	□
64	21 52	////	////	13 53	15 52	18 06	□
62	21 26	23 11	////	13 41	15 31	17 28	19 21
60	21 06	22 22	////	13 31	15 15	17 01	18 41
N 58	20 49	21 53	////	13 22	15 00	16 41	18 14
56	20 35	21 31	23 16	13 15	14 48	16 23	17 52
54	20 23	21 13	22 31	13 08	14 38	16 09	17 34
52	20 13	20 58	22 04	13 02	14 29	15 56	17 19
50	20 03	20 45	21 43	12 56	14 20	15 45	17 06
45	19 43	20 19	21 06	12 44	14 03	15 22	16 39
N 40	19 27	19 59	20 39	12 34	13 48	15 04	16 18
35	19 14	19 43	20 18	12 26	13 36	14 48	16 00
30	19 02	19 29	20 02	12 19	13 26	14 35	15 45
20	18 43	19 07	19 35	12 06	13 08	14 12	15 19
N 10	18 25	18 48	19 15	11 55	12 52	13 53	14 57
0	18 10	18 32	18 58	11 45	12 37	13 35	14 36
S 10	17 54	18 16	18 42	11 35	12 23	13 17	14 16
20	17 37	18 01	18 28	11 24	12 08	12 57	13 53
30	17 18	17 44	18 13	11 12	11 50	12 35	13 28
35	17 07	17 35	18 06	11 04	11 40	12 22	13 13
40	16 54	17 24	17 58	10 56	11 28	12 07	12 55
45	16 40	17 12	17 49	10 47	11 14	11 49	12 34
S 50	16 21	16 58	17 39	10 36	10 58	11 27	12 08
52	16 13	16 52	17 35	10 31	10 50	11 17	11 55
54	16 03	16 45	17 30	10 25	10 42	11 05	11 40
56	15 52	16 37	17 25	10 19	10 32	10 52	11 23
58	15 40	16 28	17 19	10 12	10 21	10 36	11 03
S 60	15 25	16 19	17 13	10 04	10 09	10 18	10 37

SUN and MOON

Day	SUN Eqn. of Time 00h	12h	Mer. Pass.	MOON Mer. Pass. Upper	Lower	Age	Phase
15	05 52	05 55	12 06	05 33	17 58	23	◗
16	05 58	06 01	12 06	06 25	18 52	24	
17	06 03	06 06	12 06	07 21	19 50	25	

56	SUN PLANETS	ARIES	MOON	v or Corr^n d	v or Corr^n d	v or Corr^n d
s	° ′	° ′	° ′	′ ′	′ ′	′ ′
00	14 00·0	14 02·3	13 21·7	0·0 0·0	6·0 5·7	12·0 11·3
01	14 00·3	14 02·6	13 22·0	0·1 0·1	6·1 5·7	12·1 11·4
02	14 00·5	14 02·8	13 22·2	0·2 0·2	6·2 5·8	12·2 11·5
03	14 00·8	14 03·1	13 22·4	0·3 0·3	6·3 5·9	12·3 11·6
04	14 01·0	14 03·3	13 22·7	0·4 0·4	6·4 6·0	12·4 11·7
05	14 01·3	14 03·6	13 22·9	0·5 0·5	6·5 6·1	12·5 11·8
06	14 01·5	14 03·8	13 23·2	0·6 0·6	6·6 6·2	12·6 11·9
07	14 01·8	14 04·1	13 23·4	0·7 0·7	6·7 6·3	12·7 12·0
08	14 02·0	14 04·3	13 23·6	0·8 0·8	6·8 6·4	12·8 12·1
09	14 02·3	14 04·6	13 23·9	0·9 0·8	6·9 6·5	12·9 12·1
10	14 02·5	14 04·8	13 24·1	1·0 0·9	7·0 6·6	13·0 12·2
11	14 02·8	14 05·1	13 24·4	1·1 1·0	7·1 6·7	13·1 12·3
12	14 03·0	14 05·3	13 24·6	1·2 1·1	7·2 6·8	13·2 12·4
13	14 03·3	14 05·6	13 24·8	1·3 1·2	7·3 6·9	13·3 12·5
14	14 03·5	14 05·8	13 25·1	1·4 1·3	7·4 7·0	13·4 12·8
15	14 03·8	14 06·1	13 25·3	1·5 1·4	7·5 7·1	13·5 12·7
16	14 04·0	14 06·3	13 25·6	1·6 1·5	7·6 7·2	13·6 12·8
17	14 04·3	14 06·6	13 25·8	1·7 1·6	7·7 7·3	13·7 13·1
18	14 04·5	14 06·8	13 26·0	1·8 1·7	7·8 7·3	13·8 13·0
19	14 04·8	14 07·1	13 26·3	1·9 1·8	7·9 7·4	13·9 13·1
20	14 05·0	14 07·3	13 26·5	2·0 1·9	8·0 7·5	14·0 13·2
21	14 05·3	14 07·6	13 26·7	2·1 2·0	8·1 7·6	14·1 13·3
22	14 05·5	14 07·8	13 27·0	2·2 2·1	8·2 7·7	14·2 13·4
23	14 05·8	14 08·1	13 27·2	2·3 2·2	8·3 7·8	14·3 13·5
24	14 06·0	14 08·3	13 27·5	2·4 2·3	8·4 7·9	14·4 13·6
25	14 06·3	14 08·6	13 27·7	2·5 2·4	8·5 8·0	14·5 13·7
26	14 06·5	14 08·8	13 27·9	2·6 2·5	8·6 8·1	14·6 14·0
27	14 06·8	14 09·1	13 28·2	2·7 2·5	8·7 8·2	14·7 13·8
28	14 07·0	14 09·3	13 28·4	2·8 2·6	8·8 8·3	14·8 13·9
29	14 07·3	14 09·6	13 28·7	2·9 2·7	8·9 8·4	14·9 14·0
30	14 07·5	14 09·8	13 28·9	3·0 2·8	9·0 8·5	15·0 14·1
31	14 07·8	14 10·1	13 29·1	3·1 2·9	9·1 8·6	15·1 14·2
32	14 08·0	14 10·3	13 29·4	3·2 3·0	9·2 8·7	15·2 14·3
33	14 08·3	14 10·6	13 29·6	3·3 3·1	9·3 8·8	15·3 14·4
34	14 08·5	14 10·8	13 29·8	3·4 3·2	9·4 8·9	15·4 14·5
35	14 08·8	14 11·1	13 30·1	3·5 3·3	9·5 8·9	15·5 14·6
36	14 09·0	14 11·3	13 30·3	3·6 3·4	9·6 9·0	15·6 14·7
37	14 09·3	14 11·6	13 30·6	3·7 3·5	9·7 9·1	15·7 14·8
38	14 09·5	14 11·8	13 30·8	3·8 3·6	9·8 9·2	15·8 14·9
39	14 09·8	14 12·1	13 31·0	3·9 3·7	9·9 9·3	15·9 15·0
40	14 10·0	14 12·3	13 31·3	4·0 3·8	10·0 9·4	16·0 15·1
41	14 10·3	14 12·6	13 31·5	4·1 3·9	10·1 9·5	16·1 15·2
42	14 10·5	14 12·8	13 31·8	4·2 4·0	10·2 9·6	16·2 15·3
43	14 10·8	14 13·1	13 32·0	4·3 4·0	10·3 9·7	16·3 15·4
44	14 11·0	14 13·3	13 32·2	4·4 4·1	10·4 9·8	16·4 15·4
45	14 11·3	14 13·6	13 32·5	4·5 4·2	10·5 9·9	16·5 15·5
46	14 11·5	14 13·8	13 32·7	4·6 4·3	10·6 10·0	16·6 15·6
47	14 11·8	14 14·1	13 32·9	4·7 4·4	10·7 10·1	16·7 15·7
48	14 12·0	14 14·3	13 33·2	4·8 4·5	10·8 10·2	16·8 15·8
49	14 12·3	14 14·6	13 33·4	4·9 4·6	10·9 10·3	16·9 15·9
50	14 12·5	14 14·8	13 33·7	5·0 4·7	11·0 10·4	17·0 16·0
51	14 12·8	14 15·1	13 33·9	5·1 4·8	11·1 10·5	17·1 16·1
52	14 13·0	14 15·3	13 34·1	5·2 4·9	11·2 10·5	17·2 16·2
53	14 13·3	14 15·6	13 34·4	5·3 5·0	11·3 10·6	17·3 16·3
54	14 13·5	14 15·8	13 34·6	5·4 5·1	11·4 10·7	17·4 16·7
55	14 13·8	14 16·1	13 34·9	5·5 5·2	11·5 10·8	17·5 16·5
56	14 14·0	14 16·3	13 35·1	5·6 5·3	11·6 10·9	17·6 16·6
57	14 14·3	14 16·6	13 35·3	5·7 5·4	11·7 11·0	17·7 16·7
58	14 14·5	14 16·8	13 35·6	5·8 5·5	11·8 11·1	17·8 16·8
59	14 14·8	14 17·1	13 35·8	5·9 5·6	11·9 11·2	17·9 16·9
60	14 15·0	14 17·3	13 36·1	6·0 5·7	12·0 11·3	18·0 17·0

57	SUN PLANETS	ARIES	MOON	v or Corr^n d	v or Corr^n d	v or Corr^n d
s	° ′	° ′	° ′	′ ′	′ ′	′ ′
00	14 15·0	14 17·3	13 36·1	0·0 0·0	6·0 5·8	12·0 11·5
01	14 15·3	14 17·6	13 36·3	0·1 0·1	6·1 5·8	12·1 11·6
02	14 15·5	14 17·8	13 36·5	0·2 0·2	6·2 5·9	12·2 11·7
03	14 15·8	14 18·1	13 36·8	0·3 0·3	6·3 6·0	12·3 11·8
04	14 16·0	14 18·3	13 37·0	0·4 0·4	6·4 6·1	12·4 11·9
05	14 16·3	14 18·6	13 37·2	0·5 0·5	6·5 6·2	12·5 12·0
06	14 16·5	14 18·8	13 37·5	0·6 0·6	6·6 6·3	12·6 12·1
07	14 16·8	14 19·1	13 37·7	0·7 0·7	6·7 6·4	12·7 12·2
08	14 17·0	14 19·3	13 38·0	0·8 0·8	6·8 6·5	12·8 12·3
09	14 17·3	14 19·6	13 38·2	0·9 0·9	6·9 6·6	12·9 12·4
10	14 17·5	14 19·8	13 38·4	1·0 1·0	7·0 6·7	13·0 12·5
11	14 17·8	14 20·1	13 38·7	1·1 1·1	7·1 6·8	13·1 12·6
12	14 18·0	14 20·3	13 38·9	1·2 1·2	7·2 6·9	13·2 12·7
13	14 18·3	14 20·6	13 39·2	1·3 1·2	7·3 7·0	13·3 12·7
14	14 18·5	14 20·9	13 39·4	1·4 1·3	7·4 7·1	13·4 12·8
15	14 18·8	14 21·1	13 39·6	1·5 1·4	7·5 7·2	13·5 12·9
16	14 19·0	14 21·4	13 39·9	1·6 1·5	7·6 7·3	13·6 13·0
17	14 19·3	14 21·6	13 40·1	1·7 1·6	7·7 7·4	13·7 13·1
18	14 19·5	14 21·9	13 40·3	1·8 1·7	7·8 7·5	13·8 13·2
19	14 19·8	14 22·1	13 40·6	1·9 1·8	7·9 7·6	13·9 13·3
20	14 20·0	14 22·4	13 40·8	2·0 1·9	8·0 7·7	14·0 13·4
21	14 20·3	14 22·6	13 41·1	2·1 2·0	8·1 7·8	14·1 13·5
22	14 20·5	14 22·9	13 41·3	2·2 2·1	8·2 7·9	14·2 13·6
23	14 20·8	14 23·1	13 41·5	2·3 2·2	8·3 8·0	14·3 13·7
24	14 21·0	14 23·4	13 41·8	2·4 2·3	8·4 8·1	14·4 13·8
25	14 21·3	14 23·6	13 42·0	2·5 2·4	8·5 8·1	14·5 13·9
26	14 21·5	14 23·9	13 42·3	2·6 2·5	8·6 8·2	14·6 14·0
27	14 21·8	14 24·1	13 42·5	2·7 2·6	8·7 8·3	14·7 14·1
28	14 22·0	14 24·4	13 42·7	2·8 2·7	8·8 8·4	14·8 14·2
29	14 22·3	14 24·6	13 43·0	2·9 2·8	8·9 8·5	14·9 14·3
30	14 22·5	14 24·9	13 43·2	3·0 2·9	9·0 8·6	15·0 14·4
31	14 22·8	14 25·1	13 43·4	3·1 3·0	9·1 8·7	15·1 14·5
32	14 23·0	14 25·4	13 43·7	3·2 3·1	9·2 8·8	15·2 14·6
33	14 23·3	14 25·6	13 43·9	3·3 3·2	9·3 8·9	15·3 14·7
34	14 23·5	14 25·9	13 44·2	3·4 3·3	9·4 9·0	15·4 14·8
35	14 23·8	14 26·1	13 44·4	3·5 3·4	9·5 9·1	15·5 14·9
36	14 24·0	14 26·4	13 44·6	3·6 3·5	9·6 9·2	15·6 15·0
37	14 24·3	14 26·6	13 44·9	3·7 3·5	9·7 9·3	15·7 15·0
38	14 24·5	14 26·9	13 45·1	3·8 3·6	9·8 9·4	15·8 15·1
39	14 24·8	14 27·1	13 45·4	3·9 3·7	9·9 9·5	15·9 15·2
40	14 25·0	14 27·4	13 45·6	4·0 3·8	10·0 9·6	16·0 15·3
41	14 25·3	14 27·6	13 45·8	4·1 3·9	10·1 9·7	16·1 15·4
42	14 25·5	14 27·9	13 46·1	4·2 4·0	10·2 9·8	16·2 15·5
43	14 25·8	14 28·1	13 46·3	4·3 4·1	10·3 9·9	16·3 15·6
44	14 26·0	14 28·4	13 46·5	4·4 4·2	10·4 10·0	16·4 15·7
45	14 26·3	14 28·6	13 46·8	4·5 4·3	10·5 10·1	16·5 15·8
46	14 26·5	14 28·9	13 47·0	4·6 4·4	10·6 10·2	16·6 15·9
47	14 26·8	14 29·1	13 47·3	4·7 4·5	10·7 10·3	16·7 16·0
48	14 27·0	14 29·4	13 47·5	4·8 4·6	10·8 10·4	16·8 16·1
49	14 27·3	14 29·6	13 47·7	4·9 4·7	10·9 10·4	16·9 16·2
50	14 27·5	14 29·9	13 48·0	5·0 4·8	11·0 10·5	17·0 16·3
51	14 27·8	14 30·1	13 48·2	5·1 4·9	11·1 10·6	17·1 16·4
52	14 28·0	14 30·4	13 48·5	5·2 5·0	11·2 10·7	17·2 16·5
53	14 28·3	14 30·6	13 48·7	5·3 5·1	11·3 10·8	17·3 16·6
54	14 28·5	14 30·9	13 48·9	5·4 5·2	11·4 10·9	17·4 16·7
55	14 28·8	14 31·1	13 49·2	5·5 5·3	11·5 11·0	17·5 16·8
56	14 29·0	14 31·4	13 49·4	5·6 5·4	11·6 11·1	17·6 16·9
57	14 29·3	14 31·6	13 49·7	5·7 5·5	11·7 11·2	17·7 17·0
58	14 29·5	14 31·9	13 49·9	5·8 5·6	11·8 11·3	17·8 17·1
59	14 29·8	14 32·1	13 50·1	5·9 5·7	11·9 11·4	17·9 17·2
60	14 30·0	14 32·4	13 50·4	6·0 5·8	12·0 11·5	18·0 17·3

Appendix D

A2 ALTITUDE CORRECTION TABLES 10°–90°—SUN, STARS, PLANETS

SUN

OCT.–MAR. App. Alt.	Lower Limb	Upper Limb	APR.–SEPT. App. Alt.	Lower Limb	Upper Limb
9 34	+10·8	−21·5	9 39	+10·6	−21·2
9 45	+10·9	−21·4	9 51	+10·7	−21·1
9 56	+11·0	−21·3	10 03	+10·8	−21·0
10 08	+11·1	−21·2	10 15	+10·9	−20·9
10 21	+11·2	−21·1	10 27	+11·0	−20·8
10 34	+11·3	−21·0	10 40	+11·1	−20·7
10 47	+11·4	−20·9	10 54	+11·2	−20·6
11 01	+11·5	−20·8	11 08	+11·3	−20·5
11 15	+11·6	−20·7	11 23	+11·4	−20·4
11 30	+11·7	−20·6	11 38	+11·5	−20·3
11 46	+11·8	−20·5	11 54	+11·6	−20·2
12 02	+11·9	−20·4	12 10	+11·7	−20·1
12 19	+12·0	−20·3	12 28	+11·8	−20·0
12 37	+12·1	−20·2	12 46	+11·9	−19·9
12 55	+12·2	−20·1	13 05	+12·0	−19·8
13 14	+12·3	−20·0	13 24	+12·1	−19·7
13 35	+12·4	−19·9	13 45	+12·2	−19·6
13 56	+12·5	−19·8	14 07	+12·3	−19·5
14 18	+12·6	−19·7	14 30	+12·4	−19·4
14 42	+12·7	−19·6	14 54	+12·5	−19·3
15 06	+12·8	−19·5	15 19	+12·6	−19·2
15 32	+12·9	−19·4	15 46	+12·7	−19·1
15 59	+13·0	−19·3	16 14	+12·8	−19·0
16 28	+13·1	−19·2	16 44	+12·9	−18·9
16 59	+13·2	−19·1	17 15	+13·0	−18·8
17 32	+13·3	−19·0	17 48	+13·1	−18·7
18 06	+13·4	−18·9	18 24	+13·2	−18·6
18 42	+13·5	−18·8	19 01	+13·3	−18·5
19 21	+13·6	−18·7	19 42	+13·4	−18·4
20 03	+13·7	−18·6	20 25	+13·5	−18·3
20 48	+13·8	−18·5	21 11	+13·6	−18·2
21 35	+13·9	−18·4	22 00	+13·7	−18·1
22 26	+14·0	−18·3	22 54	+13·8	−18·0
23 22	+14·1	−18·2	23 51	+13·9	−17·9
24 21	+14·2	−18·1	24 53	+14·0	−17·8
25 26	+14·3	−18·0	26 00	+14·1	−17·7
26 36	+14·4	−17·9	27 13	+14·2	−17·6
27 52	+14·5	−17·8	28 33	+14·3	−17·5
29 15	+14·6	−17·7	30 00	+14·4	−17·4
30 46	+14·7	−17·6	31 35	+14·5	−17·3
32 26	+14·8	−17·5	33 20	+14·6	−17·2
34 17	+14·9	−17·4	35 17	+14·7	−17·1
36 20	+15·0	−17·3	37 26	+14·8	−17·0
38 36	+15·1	−17·2	39 50	+14·9	−16·9
41 08	+15·2	−17·1	42 31	+15·0	−16·8
43 59	+15·3	−17·0	45 31	+15·1	−16·7
47 10	+15·4	−16·9	48 55	+15·2	−16·6
50 46	+15·5	−16·8	52 44	+15·3	−16·5
54 49	+15·6	−16·7	57 02	+15·4	−16·4
59 23	+15·7	−16·6	61 51	+15·5	−16·3
64 30	+15·8	−16·5	67 17	+15·6	−16·2
70 12	+15·9	−16·4	73 16	+15·7	−16·1
76 26	+16·0	−16·3	79 43	+15·8	−16·0
83 05	+16·1	−16·2	86 32	+15·9	−15·9
90 00			90 00		

STARS AND PLANETS

App. Alt.	Corrⁿ	App. Alt.	Additional Corrⁿ
9 56	−5·3		**1993**
10 08	−5·3		**VENUS**
10 20	−5·2		Jan. 1–Feb. 2
10 33	−5·1		May 28–July 15
10 46	−5·0		
11 00	−4·9	0	+0·2
11 14	−4·8	41	+0·1
11 29	−4·7	76	
11 45	−4·6	Feb. 3–Feb. 26	
12 01	−4·5	May 5–May 27	
12 18	−4·4		
12 35	−4·3	0	+0·3
12 54	−4·2	34	+0·2
13 13	−4·1	60	+0·1
13 33	−4·0	80	
13 54	−3·9	Feb. 27–Mar. 14	
14 16	−3·8	Apr. 19–May 4	
14 40	−3·7		
15 04	−3·6	0	+0·4
15 30	−3·5	29	+0·3
15 57	−3·4	51	+0·2
16 26	−3·3	68	+0·1
16 56	−3·2	83	
17 28	−3·1	Mar. 15–Apr. 18	
18 02	−3·0		
18 38	−2·9	0	+0·5
19 17	−2·8	26	+0·4
19 58	−2·7	46	+0·3
20 42	−2·6	60	+0·2
21 28	−2·5	73	+0·1
22 19	−2·4	84	
23 13	−2·3	July 16–Dec. 31	
24 11	−2·2		
25 14	−2·1	0	+0·1
26 22	−2·0	60	
27 36	−1·9	**MARS**	
28 56	−1·8	Jan. 1–Mar. 7	
30 24	−1·7		
32 00	−1·6	0	+0·2
33 45	−1·5	41	+0·1
35 40	−1·4	76	
37 48	−1·3	Mar. 8–Dec. 31	
40 08	−1·2		
42 44	−1·1	0	+0·1
45 36	−1·0	60	
48 47	−0·9		
52 18	−0·8		
56 11	−0·7		
60 28	−0·6		
65 08	−0·5		
70 11	−0·4		
75 34	−0·3		
81 13	−0·2		
87 03	−0·1		
90 00	0·0		

DIP

Ht. of Eye (m)	Corrⁿ	Ht. of Eye (ft)	Ht. of Eye (m)	Corrⁿ
2·4	−2·8	8·0	1·0	−1·8
2·6	−2·9	8·6	1·5	−2·2
2·8	−2·9	9·2	2·0	−2·5
3·0	−3·0	9·8	2·5	−2·8
3·2	−3·1	10·5	3·0	−3·0
3·4	−3·2	11·2	See table	
3·6	−3·3	11·9	←	
3·8	−3·4	12·6		
4·0	−3·5	13·3	m 20	−7·9
4·3	−3·6	14·1	22	−8·3
4·5	−3·7	14·9	24	−8·6
4·7	−3·8	15·7	26	−9·0
5·0	−3·9	16·5	28	−9·3
5·2	−4·0	17·4		
5·5	−4·1	18·3	30	−9·6
5·8	−4·2	19·1	32	−10·0
6·1	−4·3	20·1	34	−10·3
6·3	−4·4	21·0	36	−10·6
6·6	−4·5	22·0	38	−10·8
6·9	−4·6	22·9		
7·2	−4·7	23·9	40	−11·1
7·5	−4·8	24·9	42	−11·4
7·9	−4·9	26·0	44	−11·7
8·2	−5·0	27·1	46	−11·9
8·5	−5·1	28·1	48	−12·2
8·8	−5·2	29·2		
9·2	−5·3	30·4	ft.	
9·5	−5·4	31·5	2	−1·4
9·9	−5·5	32·7	4	−1·9
10·3	−5·6	33·9	6	−2·4
10·6	−5·7	35·1	8	−2·7
11·0	−5·8	36·3	10	−3·1
11·4	−5·9	37·6	See table	
11·8	−6·0	38·9	←	
12·2	−6·1	40·1	ft.	
12·6	−6·2	41·5	70	−8·1
13·0	−6·3	42·8	75	−8·4
13·4	−6·4	44·2	80	−8·7
13·8	−6·5	45·5	85	−8·9
14·2	−6·6	46·9	90	−9·2
14·7	−6·7	48·4	95	−9·5
15·1	−6·8	49·8		
15·5	−6·9	51·3	100	−9·7
16·0	−7·0	52·8	105	−9·9
16·5	−7·1	54·3	110	−10·2
16·9	−7·2	55·8	115	−10·4
17·4	−7·3	57·4	120	−10·6
17·9	−7·4	58·9	125	−10·8
18·4	−7·5	60·5		
18·8	−7·6	62·1	130	−11·1
19·3	−7·7	63·8	135	−11·3
19·8	−7·8	65·4	140	−11·5
20·4	−7·9	67·1	145	−11·7
20·9	−8·0	68·8	150	−11·9
21·4	−8·1	70·5	155	−12·1

App. Alt. = Apparent altitude = Sextant altitude corrected for index error and dip.

Appendix E

ALTITUDE CORRECTION TABLES 0°–35°—MOON

App. Alt.	0°–4° Corrⁿ	5°–9° Corrⁿ	10°–14° Corrⁿ	15°–19° Corrⁿ	20°–24° Corrⁿ	25°–29° Corrⁿ	30°–34° Corrⁿ	App. Alt.
00	0 33·8	5 58·2	10 62·1	15 62·8	20 62·2	25 60·8	30 58·9	00
10	35·9	58·5	62·2	62·8	62·1	60·8	58·8	10
20	37·8	58·7	62·2	62·8	62·1	60·7	58·8	20
30	39·6	58·9	62·3	62·8	62·1	60·7	58·7	30
40	41·2	59·1	62·3	62·8	62·0	60·6	58·6	40
50	42·6	59·3	62·4	62·7	62·0	60·6	58·5	50
00	1 44·0	6 59·5	11 62·4	16 62·7	21 62·0	26 60·5	31 58·5	00
10	45·2	59·7	62·4	62·7	61·9	60·4	58·4	10
20	46·3	59·9	62·5	62·7	61·9	60·4	58·3	20
30	47·3	60·0	62·5	62·7	61·9	60·3	58·2	30
40	48·3	60·2	62·5	62·7	61·8	60·3	58·2	40
50	49·2	60·3	62·6	62·7	61·8	60·2	58·1	50
00	2 50·0	7 60·5	12 62·6	17 62·7	22 61·7	27 60·1	32 58·0	00
10	50·8	60·6	62·6	62·6	61·7	60·1	57·9	10
20	51·4	60·7	62·6	62·6	61·6	60·0	57·8	20
30	52·1	60·9	62·7	62·6	61·6	59·9	57·8	30
40	52·7	61·0	62·7	62·6	61·5	59·9	57·7	40
50	53·3	61·1	62·7	62·6	61·5	59·8	57·6	50
00	3 53·8	8 61·2	13 62·7	18 62·5	23 61·5	28 59·7	33 57·5	00
10	54·3	61·3	62·7	62·5	61·4	59·7	57·4	10
20	54·8	61·4	62·7	62·5	61·4	59·6	57·4	20
30	55·2	61·5	62·8	62·4	61·3	59·6	57·3	30
40	55·6	61·6	62·8	62·4	61·3	59·5	57·2	40
50	56·0	61·6	62·8	62·4	61·2	59·4	57·1	50
00	4 56·4	9 61·7	14 62·8	19 62·4	24 61·2	29 59·3	34 57·0	00
10	56·7	61·8	62·8	62·3	61·1	59·3	56·9	10
20	57·1	61·9	62·8	62·3	61·1	59·2	56·9	20
30	57·4	61·9	62·8	62·3	61·0	59·1	56·8	30
40	57·7	62·0	62·8	62·2	60·9	59·1	56·7	40
50	57·9	62·1	62·8	62·2	60·9	59·0	56·6	50

H.P.	L U	L U	L U	L U	L U	L U	L U	H.P.
54·0	0·3 0·9	0·3 0·9	0·4 1·0	0·5 1·1	0·6 1·2	0·7 1·3	0·9 1·5	54·0
54·3	0·7 1·1	0·7 1·2	0·7 1·2	0·8 1·3	0·9 1·4	1·1 1·5	1·2 1·7	54·3
54·6	1·1 1·4	1·1 1·4	1·1 1·4	1·2 1·5	1·3 1·6	1·4 1·7	1·5 1·8	54·6
54·9	1·4 1·6	1·5 1·6	1·5 1·6	1·6 1·7	1·6 1·8	1·8 1·9	1·9 2·0	54·9
55·2	1·8 1·8	1·8 1·8	1·9 1·9	1·9 1·9	2·0 2·0	2·1 2·1	2·2 2·2	55·2
55·5	2·2 2·0	2·2 2·0	2·3 2·1	2·3 2·1	2·4 2·2	2·4 2·3	2·5 2·4	55·5
55·8	2·6 2·2	2·6 2·2	2·6 2·3	2·7 2·3	2·7 2·4	2·8 2·4	2·9 2·5	55·8
56·1	3·0 2·4	3·0 2·5	3·0 2·5	3·0 2·5	3·1 2·6	3·1 2·6	3·2 2·7	56·1
56·4	3·4 2·7	3·4 2·7	3·4 2·7	3·4 2·7	3·4 2·8	3·5 2·8	3·5 2·9	56·4
56·7	3·7 2·9	3·7 2·9	3·8 2·9	3·8 2·9	3·8 3·0	3·8 3·0	3·9 3·0	56·7
57·0	4·1 3·1	4·1 3·1	4·1 3·1	4·1 3·1	4·2 3·1	4·2 3·2	4·2 3·2	57·0
57·3	4·5 3·3	4·5 3·3	4·5 3·3	4·5 3·3	4·5 3·4	4·5 3·4	4·6 3·4	57·3
57·6	4·9 3·5	4·9 3·5	4·9 3·5	4·9 3·5	4·9 3·5	4·9 3·5	4·9 3·6	57·6
57·9	5·3 3·8	5·3 3·8	5·2 3·8	5·2 3·7	5·2 3·7	5·2 3·7	5·2 3·7	57·9
58·2	5·6 4·0	5·6 4·0	5·6 4·0	5·6 4·0	5·6 3·9	5·6 3·9	5·6 3·9	58·2
58·5	6·0 4·2	6·0 4·2	6·0 4·2	6·0 4·2	6·0 4·1	5·9 4·1	5·9 4·1	58·5
58·8	6·4 4·4	6·4 4·4	6·4 4·4	6·3 4·4	6·3 4·3	6·3 4·3	6·2 4·2	58·8
59·1	6·8 4·6	6·8 4·6	6·7 4·6	6·7 4·6	6·7 4·5	6·6 4·5	6·6 4·4	59·1
59·4	7·2 4·8	7·1 4·8	7·1 4·8	7·1 4·8	7·0 4·7	7·0 4·7	6·9 4·6	59·4
59·7	7·5 5·1	7·5 5·0	7·5 5·0	7·5 5·0	7·4 4·9	7·3 4·8	7·2 4·7	59·7
60·0	7·9 5·3	7·9 5·3	7·9 5·2	7·8 5·2	7·8 5·1	7·7 5·0	7·6 4·9	60·0
60·3	8·3 5·5	8·3 5·5	8·2 5·4	8·2 5·4	8·1 5·3	8·0 5·2	7·9 5·1	60·3
60·6	8·7 5·7	8·7 5·7	8·6 5·7	8·6 5·6	8·5 5·5	8·4 5·4	8·2 5·3	60·6
60·9	9·1 5·9	9·0 5·9	9·0 5·9	8·9 5·8	8·8 5·7	8·7 5·6	8·6 5·4	60·9
61·2	9·5 6·2	9·4 6·1	9·4 6·1	9·3 6·0	9·2 5·9	9·1 5·8	8·9 5·6	61·2
61·5	9·8 6·4	9·8 6·3	9·7 6·3	9·7 6·2	9·5 6·1	9·4 5·9	9·2 5·8	61·5

DIP

Ht. of Eye (m)	Corrⁿ	Ht. of Eye (ft.)	Ht. of Eye (m)	Corrⁿ	Ht. of Eye (ft.)
2·4	−2·8	8·0	9·5	−5·5	31·5
2·6	−2·9	8·6	9·9	−5·6	32·7
2·8	−3·0	9·2	10·3	−5·7	33·9
3·0	−3·1	9·8	10·6	−5·8	35·1
3·2	−3·2	10·5	11·0	−5·9	36·3
3·4	−3·3	11·2	11·4	−6·0	37·6
3·6	−3·4	11·9	11·8	−6·1	38·9
3·8	−3·5	12·6	12·2	−6·2	40·1
4·0	−3·6	13·3	12·6	−6·3	41·5
4·3	−3·7	14·1	13·0	−6·4	42·8
4·5	−3·8	14·9	13·4	−6·5	44·2
4·7	−3·9	15·7	13·8	−6·6	45·5
5·0	−4·0	16·5	14·2	−6·7	46·9
5·2	−4·1	17·4	14·7	−6·8	48·4
5·5	−4·2	18·3	15·1	−6·9	49·8
5·8	−4·3	19·1	15·5	−7·0	51·3
6·1	−4·4	20·1	16·0	−7·1	52·8
6·3	−4·5	21·0	16·5	−7·2	54·3
6·6	−4·6	22·0	16·9	−7·3	55·8
6·9	−4·7	22·9	17·4	−7·4	57·4
7·2	−4·8	23·9	17·9	−7·5	58·9
7·5	−4·9	24·9	18·4	−7·6	60·5
7·9	−5·0	26·0	18·8	−7·7	62·1
8·2	−5·1	27·1	19·3	−7·8	63·8
8·5	−5·2	28·1	19·8	−7·9	65·4
8·8	−5·3	29·2	20·4	−8·0	67·1
9·2	−5·4	30·4	20·9	−8·1	68·8
9·5		31·5	21·4		70·5

MOON CORRECTION TABLE

The correction is in two parts; the first correction is taken from the upper part of the table with argument apparent altitude, and the second from the lower part, with argument H.P., in the same column as that from which the first correction was taken. Separate corrections are given in the lower part for lower (L) and upper (U) limbs. All corrections are to be **added** to apparent altitude, but 30′ is to be subtracted from the altitude of the upper limb.

For corrections for pressure and temperature see page A4.

For bubble sextant observations ignore dip, take the mean of upper and lower limb corrections and subtract 15′ from the altitude.

App. Alt. = Apparent altitude = Sextant altitude corrected for index error and dip.

Appendix E

ALTITUDE CORRECTION TABLES 35°–90°—MOON

App. Alt.	35°–39° Corrⁿ	40°–44° Corrⁿ	45°–49° Corrⁿ	50°–54° Corrⁿ	55°–59° Corrⁿ	60°–64° Corrⁿ	65°–69° Corrⁿ	70°–74° Corrⁿ	75°–79° Corrⁿ	80°–84° Corrⁿ	85°–89° Corrⁿ	App. Alt.
00	35 56·5	40 53·7	45 50·5	50 46·9	55 43·1	60 38·9	65 34·6	70 30·1	75 25·3	80 20·5	85 15·6	00
10	56·4	53·6	50·4	46·8	42·9	38·8	34·4	29·9	25·2	20·4	15·5	10
20	56·3	53·5	50·2	46·7	42·8	38·7	34·3	29·7	25·0	20·2	15·3	20
30	56·2	53·4	50·1	46·5	42·7	38·5	34·1	29·6	24·9	20·0	15·1	30
40	56·2	53·3	50·0	46·4	42·5	38·4	34·0	29·4	24·7	19·9	15·0	40
50	56·1	53·2	49·9	46·3	42·4	38·2	33·8	29·3	24·5	19·7	14·8	50
00	36 56·0	41 53·1	46 49·8	51 46·2	56 42·3	61 38·1	66 33·7	71 29·1	76 24·4	81 19·6	86 14·6	00
10	55·9	53·0	49·7	46·0	42·1	37·9	33·5	29·0	24·2	19·4	14·5	10
20	55·8	52·8	49·5	45·9	42·0	37·8	33·4	28·8	24·1	19·2	14·3	20
30	55·7	52·7	49·4	45·8	41·8	37·7	33·2	28·7	23·9	19·1	14·1	30
40	55·6	52·6	49·3	45·7	41·7	37·5	33·1	28·5	23·8	18·9	14·0	40
50	55·5	52·5	49·2	45·5	41·6	37·4	32·9	28·3	23·6	18·7	13·8	50
00	37 55·4	42 52·4	47 49·1	52 45·4	57 41·4	62 37·2	67 32·8	72 28·2	77 23·4	82 18·6	87 13·7	00
10	55·3	52·3	49·0	45·3	41·3	37·1	32·6	28·0	23·3	18·4	13·5	10
20	55·2	52·2	48·8	45·2	41·2	36·9	32·5	27·9	23·1	18·2	13·3	20
30	55·1	52·1	48·7	45·0	41·0	36·8	32·3	27·7	22·9	18·1	13·2	30
40	55·0	52·0	48·6	44·9	40·9	36·6	32·2	27·6	22·8	17·9	13·0	40
50	55·0	51·9	48·5	44·8	40·8	36·5	32·0	27·4	22·6	17·8	12·8	50
00	38 54·9	43 51·8	48 48·4	53 44·6	58 40·6	63 36·4	68 31·9	73 27·2	78 22·5	83 17·6	88 12·7	00
10	54·8	51·7	48·2	44·5	40·5	36·2	31·7	27·1	22·3	17·4	12·5	10
20	54·7	51·6	48·1	44·4	40·3	36·1	31·6	26·9	22·1	17·3	12·3	20
30	54·6	51·5	48·0	44·2	40·2	35·9	31·4	26·8	22·0	17·1	12·2	30
40	54·5	51·4	47·9	44·1	40·1	35·8	31·3	26·6	21·8	16·9	12·0	40
50	54·4	51·2	47·8	44·0	39·9	35·6	31·1	26·5	21·7	16·8	11·8	50
00	39 54·3	44 51·1	49 47·6	54 43·9	59 39·8	64 35·5	69 31·0	74 26·3	79 21·5	84 16·6	89 11·7	00
10	54·2	51·0	47·5	43·7	39·6	35·3	30·8	26·1	21·3	16·5	11·5	10
20	54·1	50·9	47·4	43·6	39·5	35·2	30·7	26·0	21·2	16·3	11·4	20
30	54·0	50·8	47·3	43·5	39·4	35·0	30·5	25·8	21·0	16·1	11·2	30
40	53·9	50·7	47·2	43·3	39·2	34·9	30·4	25·7	20·9	16·0	11·0	40
50	53·8	50·6	47·0	43·2	39·1	34·7	30·2	25·5	20·7	15·8	10·9	50

H.P.	L U	L U	L U	L U	L U	L U	L U	L U	L U	L U	L U	H.P.
54·0	1·1 1·7	1·3 1·9	1·5 2·1	1·7 2·4	2·0 2·6	2·3 2·9	2·6 3·2	2·9 3·5	3·2 3·8	3·5 4·1	3·8 4·5	54·0
54·3	1·4 1·8	1·6 2·0	1·8 2·2	2·0 2·5	2·3 2·7	2·5 3·0	2·8 3·2	3·0 3·5	3·3 3·8	3·6 4·1	3·9 4·4	54·3
54·6	1·7 2·0	1·9 2·2	2·1 2·4	2·3 2·6	2·5 2·8	2·7 3·0	3·0 3·3	3·2 3·5	3·5 3·8	3·7 4·1	4·0 4·3	54·6
54·9	2·0 2·2	2·2 2·3	2·3 2·5	2·5 2·7	2·7 2·9	2·9 3·1	3·2 3·3	3·4 3·5	3·6 3·8	3·9 4·0	4·1 4·3	54·9
55·2	2·3 2·3	2·5 2·4	2·6 2·6	2·8 2·8	3·0 2·9	3·2 3·1	3·4 3·3	3·6 3·5	3·8 3·7	4·0 4·0	4·2 4·2	55·2
55·5	2·7 2·5	2·8 2·6	2·9 2·7	3·1 2·9	3·2 3·0	3·4 3·2	3·6 3·4	3·7 3·5	3·9 3·7	4·1 3·9	4·3 4·1	55·5
55·8	3·0 2·6	3·1 2·7	3·2 2·8	3·3 3·0	3·5 3·1	3·6 3·3	3·8 3·4	3·9 3·6	4·1 3·7	4·2 3·9	4·3 4·0	55·8
56·1	3·3 2·8	3·4 2·9	3·5 3·0	3·6 3·1	3·7 3·2	3·8 3·3	4·0 3·4	4·1 3·6	4·2 3·7	4·4 3·8	4·5 4·0	56·1
56·4	3·6 2·9	3·7 3·0	3·8 3·1	3·9 3·2	3·9 3·3	4·0 3·4	4·1 3·5	4·3 3·6	4·4 3·7	4·5 3·8	4·6 3·9	56·4
56·7	3·9 3·1	4·0 3·1	4·1 3·2	4·1 3·3	4·2 3·3	4·3 3·4	4·3 3·5	4·4 3·6	4·5 3·7	4·6 3·8	4·7 3·8	56·7
57·0	4·3 3·2	4·3 3·3	4·3 3·3	4·4 3·4	4·4 3·4	4·5 3·5	4·5 3·5	4·6 3·6	4·7 3·6	4·7 3·7	4·8 3·8	57·0
57·3	4·6 3·4	4·6 3·4	4·6 3·4	4·6 3·5	4·7 3·5	4·7 3·5	4·7 3·6	4·8 3·6	4·8 3·6	4·8 3·7	4·9 3·7	57·3
57·6	4·9 3·6	4·9 3·6	4·9 3·6	4·9 3·6	4·9 3·6	4·9 3·6	4·9 3·6	4·9 3·6	5·0 3·6	5·0 3·6	5·0 3·6	57·6
57·9	5·2 3·7	5·2 3·7	5·2 3·7	5·2 3·7	5·2 3·7	5·1 3·6	5·1 3·6	5·1 3·6	5·1 3·6	5·1 3·6	5·1 3·5	57·9
58·2	5·5 3·9	5·5 3·8	5·5 3·8	5·4 3·8	5·4 3·7	5·4 3·7	5·3 3·7	5·3 3·6	5·2 3·6	5·2 3·5	5·2 3·5	58·2
58·5	5·9 4·0	5·8 4·0	5·8 3·9	5·7 3·9	5·6 3·8	5·6 3·8	5·5 3·7	5·5 3·6	5·4 3·6	5·3 3·5	5·3 3·4	58·5
58·8	6·2 4·2	6·1 4·1	6·0 4·1	6·0 4·0	5·9 3·9	5·8 3·8	5·7 3·7	5·6 3·6	5·5 3·5	5·4 3·5	5·3 3·4	58·8
59·1	6·5 4·3	6·4 4·3	6·4 4·2	6·2 4·1	6·1 4·0	6·0 3·9	5·9 3·8	5·8 3·6	5·7 3·5	5·4 3·5	5·3 3·3	59·1
59·4	6·8 4·5	6·7 4·4	6·6 4·3	6·5 4·2	6·4 4·1	6·2 3·9	6·1 3·8	6·0 3·7	5·8 3·5	5·7 3·4	5·5 3·2	59·4
59·7	7·1 4·6	7·0 4·5	6·9 4·4	6·8 4·3	6·6 4·1	6·5 4·0	6·3 3·8	6·2 3·7	6·0 3·5	5·8 3·3	5·6 3·2	59·7
60·0	7·5 4·8	7·3 4·7	7·2 4·5	7·0 4·4	6·9 4·2	6·7 4·0	6·5 3·9	6·3 3·7	6·1 3·5	5·9 3·3	5·7 3·1	60·0
60·3	7·8 5·0	7·6 4·8	7·4 4·7	7·3 4·5	7·1 4·3	6·9 4·1	6·7 3·9	6·5 3·7	6·3 3·5	6·0 3·2	5·8 3·0	60·3
60·6	8·1 5·1	7·9 5·0	7·7 4·8	7·6 4·6	7·3 4·4	7·1 4·2	6·9 3·9	6·7 3·7	6·4 3·4	6·2 3·2	5·9 2·9	60·6
60·9	8·4 5·3	8·2 5·1	8·0 4·9	7·8 4·7	7·6 4·5	7·3 4·2	7·1 4·0	6·8 3·7	6·6 3·4	6·3 3·2	6·0 2·9	60·9
61·2	8·7 5·4	8·5 5·2	8·3 5·0	8·1 4·8	7·8 4·5	7·6 4·3	7·3 4·0	7·0 3·7	6·7 3·4	6·4 3·1	6·1 2·8	61·2
61·5	9·1 5·6	8·8 5·4	8·6 5·1	8·3 4·9	8·1 4·6	7·8 4·3	7·5 4·0	7·2 3·7	6·9 3·4	6·5 3·1	6·2 2·7	61·5

Appendix F

LAT 52°

| 15° | 16° | 17° | 18° | 19° | 20° | 22° | 23° | 24° | 25° | 26° | 27° | 28° | 29° |

DECLINATION (15°–29°) CONTRARY NAME TO LATITUDE

LAT 52°

Appendix G

TABLE 5.—Correction to Tabulated Altitude for Minutes of Declination

d	1	2	3	4	5	6	7	8	9 10	11	12	13	14 15	16	17	18 19	20 21	22 23	24 25	26	27 28	29 30	31 32 33	34 35 36	37 38 39	40 41 42	43 44 45	46 47 48	49 50 51	52 53 54	55 56 57	58 59 60	d
0	0	0	0	0	0	0	0	0	0 0	0	0	0	0 0	0	0	0 0	0 0	0 0	0 0	0	0 0	0 0	0 0 0	0 0 0	0 0 0	0 0 0	0 0 0	0 0 0	0 0 0	0 1 1	1 1 1	1 1 1	0

198

1993 OCTOBER 10, 11, 12 (SUN., MON., TUES.)

UT (GMT)	ARIES G.H.A.	VENUS −3.9 G.H.A.	Dec.	MARS +1.6 G.H.A.	Dec.	JUPITER −1.7 G.H.A.	Dec.	SATURN +0.6 G.H.A.	Dec.	STARS Name	S.H.A.	Dec.
10 00	18 36.6	204 52.3 N 4 15.4		162 14.0 S14 29.6		176 43.2 S 8 01.7		51 51.6 S14 59.3		Acamar	315 29.1	S40 19.6
01	33 39.0	219 51.9	14.3	177 14.8	30.1	191 45.2	01.9	66 54.2	59.3	Achernar	335 37.1	S57 15.9
02	48 41.5	234 51.5	13.1	192 15.6	30.7	206 47.1	02.1	81 56.7	59.4	Acrux	173 26.5	S63 03.9
03	63 44.0	249 51.1 ··	11.9	207 16.4 ··	31.3	221 49.1 ··	02.3	96 59.2 ··	59.4	Adhara	255 24.1	S28 57.6
04	78 46.4	264 50.7	10.7	222 17.2	31.9	236 51.1	02.5	112 01.8	59.4	Aldebaran	291 06.1	N16 29.9
05	93 48.9	279 50.3	09.5	237 18.0	32.4	251 53.0	02.7	127 04.3	59.4			
06	108 51.4	294 49.9 N 4 08.4		252 18.8 S14 33.0		266 55.0 S 8 02.9		142 06.9 S14 59.5		Alioth	166 34.1	N55 59.6
07	123 53.8	309 49.5	07.2	267 19.6	33.6	281 56.9	03.1	157 09.4	59.5	Alkaid	153 10.9	N49 20.7
08	138 56.3	324 49.1	06.0	282 20.4	34.2	296 58.9	03.3	172 11.9	59.5	Al Na'ir	28 01.8	S46 59.5
S 09	153 58.8	339 48.7 ··	04.8	297 21.2 ··	34.7	312 00.8 ··	03.5	187 14.5 ··	59.5	Alnilam	276 01.2	S 1 12.2
U 10	169 01.2	354 48.3	03.6	312 22.0	35.3	327 02.8	03.7	202 17.0	59.5	Alphard	218 10.7	S 8 37.8
N 11	184 03.7	9 48.0	02.5	327 22.8	35.9	342 04.8	03.9	217 19.5	59.6			
D 12	199 06.1	24 47.6 N 4 01.3		342 23.5 S14 36.4		357 06.7 S 8 04.1		232 22.1 S14 59.6		Alphecca	126 23.8	N26 44.3
A 13	214 08.6	39 47.2 4 00.1		357 24.3	37.0	12 08.7	04.3	247 24.6	59.6	Alpheratz	357 58.4	N29 03.6
Y 14	229 11.1	54 46.8 3 58.9		12 25.1	37.6	27 10.6	04.5	262 27.2	59.6	Altair	62 22.5	N 8 51.4
15	244 13.5	69 46.4 ··	57.7	27 25.9 ··	38.2	42 12.6 ··	04.7	277 29.7 ··	59.7	Ankaa	353 29.7	S42 20.3
16	259 16.0	84 46.0	56.6	42 26.7	38.7	57 14.5	04.9	292 32.2	59.7	Antares	112 44.6	S26 25.1
17	274 18.5	99 45.6	55.4	57 27.5	39.3	72 16.5	05.1	307 34.8	59.7			
18	289 20.9	114 45.2 N 3 54.2		72 28.3 S14 39.9		87 18.4 S 8 05.3		322 37.3 S14 59.7		Arcturus	146 09.5	N19 13.0
19	304 23.4	129 44.8	53.0	87 29.1	40.5	102 20.4	05.5	337 39.8	59.7	Atria	108 00.0	S69 01.2
20	319 25.9	144 44.4	51.8	102 29.9	41.0	117 22.4	05.7	352 42.4	59.8	Avior	234 24.2	S59 29.1
21	334 28.3	159 44.0 ··	50.6	117 30.6 ··	41.6	132 24.3 ··	05.9	7 44.9 ··	59.8	Bellatrix	278 47.6	N 6 20.7
22	349 30.8	174 43.6	49.5	132 31.4	42.2	147 26.3	06.1	22 47.4	59.8	Betelgeuse	271 17.1	N 7 24.4
23	4 33.2	189 43.2	48.3	147 32.2	42.7	162 28.2	06.4	37 50.0	59.8			
11 00	19 35.7	204 42.8 N 3 47.1		162 33.0 S14 43.3		177 30.2 S 8 06.6		52 52.5 S14 59.9		Canopus	264 02.5	S52 41.3
01	34 38.2	219 42.4	45.9	177 33.8	43.9	192 32.1	06.8	67 55.0	59.9	Capella	280 56.0	N45 59.4
02	49 40.6	234 42.1	44.7	192 34.6	44.4	207 34.1	07.0	82 57.6	59.9	Deneb	49 41.4	N45 15.9
03	64 43.1	249 41.7 ··	43.5	207 35.4 ··	45.0	222 36.1 ··	07.2	98 00.1 ··	59.9	Denebola	182 48.9	N14 36.4
04	79 45.6	264 41.3	42.3	222 36.2	45.6	237 38.0	07.4	113 02.7 14 59.9		Diphda	349 10.3	S18 01.0
05	94 48.0	279 40.9	41.2	237 36.9	46.2	252 40.0	07.6	128 05.2 15 00.0				
06	109 50.5	294 40.5 N 3 40.0		252 37.7 S14 46.7		267 41.9 S 8 07.8		143 07.7 S15 00.0		Dubhe	194 10.2	N61 46.9
07	124 53.0	309 40.1	38.8	267 38.5	47.3	282 43.9	08.0	158 10.3	00.0	Elnath	278 31.1	N28 36.1
08	139 55.4	324 39.7	37.6	282 39.3	47.9	297 45.8	08.2	173 12.8	00.0	Eltanin	90 53.2	N51 29.7
M 09	154 57.9	339 39.3 ··	36.4	297 40.1 ··	48.4	312 47.8 ··	08.4	188 15.3 ··	00.0	Enif	34 01.4	N 9 51.1
O 10	170 00.4	354 38.9	35.2	312 40.9	49.0	327 49.7	08.6	203 17.9	00.1	Fomalhaut	15 39.9	S29 39.2
N 11	185 02.8	9 38.5	34.0	327 41.6	49.6	342 51.7	08.8	218 20.4	00.1			
D 12	200 05.3	24 38.1 N 3 32.9		342 42.4 S14 50.1		357 53.7 S 8 09.0		233 22.9 S15 00.1		Gacrux	172 18.0	S57 04.7
A 13	215 07.7	39 37.7	31.7	357 43.2	50.7	12 55.6	09.2	248 25.5	00.1	Gienah	176 07.8	S17 30.4
Y 14	230 10.2	54 37.3	30.5	12 44.0	51.3	27 57.6	09.4	263 28.0	00.2	Hadar	149 09.5	S60 20.6
15	245 12.7	69 36.9 ··	29.3	27 44.8 ··	51.8	42 59.5 ··	09.6	278 30.5 ··	00.2	Hamal	328 17.1	N23 26.1
16	260 15.1	84 36.6	28.1	42 45.6	52.4	58 01.5	09.8	293 33.1	00.2	Kaus Aust.	84 03.4	S34 23.3
17	275 17.6	99 36.2	26.9	57 46.3	53.0	73 03.4	10.0	308 35.6	00.2			
18	290 20.1	114 35.8 N 3 25.7		72 47.1 S14 53.6		88 05.4 S 8 10.2		323 38.1 S15 00.2		Kochab	137 20.4	N74 11.0
19	305 22.5	129 35.4	24.5	87 47.9	54.1	103 07.3	10.4	338 40.6	00.3	Markab	13 52.7	N15 10.6
20	320 25.0	144 35.0	23.3	102 48.7	54.7	118 09.3	10.6	353 43.2	00.3	Menkar	314 30.2	N 4 04.1
21	335 27.5	159 34.6 ··	22.2	117 49.5 ··	55.3	133 11.3 ··	10.8	8 45.7 ··	00.3	Menkent	148 25.4	S36 20.4
22	350 29.9	174 34.2	21.0	132 50.2	55.8	148 13.2	11.0	23 48.2	00.3	Miaplacidus	221 43.2	S69 41.3
23	5 32.4	189 33.8	19.8	147 51.0	56.4	163 15.2	11.2	38 50.8	00.3			
12 00	20 34.9	204 33.4 N 3 18.6		162 51.8 S14 57.0		178 17.1 S 8 11.4		53 53.3 S15 00.4		Mirfak	309 01.1	N49 50.3
01	35 37.3	219 33.0	17.4	177 52.6	57.5	193 19.1	11.6	68 55.8	00.4	Nunki	76 16.6	S26 18.2
02	50 39.8	234 32.6	16.2	192 53.4	58.1	208 21.0	11.8	83 58.4	00.4	Peacock	53 42.2	S56 45.4
03	65 42.2	249 32.2 ··	15.0	207 54.2 ··	58.7	223 23.0 ··	12.0	99 00.9 ··	00.4	Pollux	243 45.7	N28 02.4
04	80 44.7	264 31.8	13.8	222 54.9	59.2	238 24.9	12.2	114 03.4	00.4	Procyon	245 15.1	N 5 14.5
05	95 47.2	279 31.5	12.6	237 55.7 14 59.8		253 26.9	12.4	129 06.0	00.5			
06	110 49.6	294 31.1 N 3 11.4		252 56.5 S15 00.3		268 28.8 S 8 12.6		144 08.5 S15 00.5		Rasalhague	96 20.3	N12 34.1
07	125 52.1	309 30.7	10.2	267 57.3	00.9	283 30.8	12.8	159 11.0	00.5	Regulus	207 59.4	N11 59.8
T 08	140 54.6	324 30.3	09.1	282 58.0	01.5	298 32.8	13.0	174 13.5	00.5	Rigel	281 26.0	S 8 12.4
U 09	155 57.0	339 29.9 ··	07.9	297 58.8 ··	02.0	313 34.7 ··	13.2	189 16.1 ··	00.5	Rigil Kent.	140 12.5	S60 48.6
E 10	170 59.5	354 29.5	06.7	312 59.6	02.6	328 36.7	13.4	204 18.6	00.6	Sabik	102 29.6	S15 43.0
S 11	186 02.0	9 29.1	05.5	328 00.4	03.2	343 38.6	13.6	219 21.1	00.6			
D 12	201 04.4	24 28.7 N 3 04.3		343 01.2 S15 03.7		358 40.6 S 8 13.8		234 23.7 S15 00.6		Schedar	349 56.8	N56 30.4
A 13	216 06.9	39 28.3	03.1	358 01.9	04.3	13 42.5	14.0	249 26.2	00.6	Shaula	96 42.1	S37 06.0
Y 14	231 09.4	54 27.9	01.9	13 02.7	04.9	28 44.5	14.2	264 28.7	00.6	Sirius	258 46.6	S16 42.3
15	246 11.8	69 27.5 3 00.7		28 03.5 ··	05.4	43 46.4 ··	14.4	279 31.3 ··	00.7	Spica	158 47.1	S11 07.7
16	261 14.3	84 27.1 2 59.5		43 04.3	06.0	58 48.4	14.6	294 33.8	00.7	Suhail	223 03.5	S43 24.3
17	276 16.7	99 26.8	58.3	58 05.0	06.6	73 50.4	14.8	309 36.3	00.7			
18	291 19.2	114 26.4 N 2 57.1		73 05.8 S15 07.1		88 52.3 S 8 15.0		324 38.8 S15 00.7		Vega	80 49.0	N38 47.0
19	306 21.7	129 26.0	55.9	88 06.6	07.7	103 54.3	15.2	339 41.4	00.7	Zuben'ubi	137 22.0	S16 00.9
20	321 24.1	144 25.6	54.7	103 07.4	08.2	118 56.2	15.4	354 43.9	00.7		S.H.A.	Mer. Pass.
21	336 26.6	159 25.2 ··	53.5	118 08.1 ··	08.8	133 58.2 ··	15.6	9 46.4 ··	00.8	Venus	185 07.1	10 21
22	351 29.1	174 24.8	52.3	133 08.9	09.4	149 00.1	15.8	24 48.9	00.8	Mars	142 57.3	13 09
23	6 31.5	189 24.4	51.2	148 09.7	09.9	164 02.1	16.0	39 51.5	00.8	Jupiter	157 54.5	12 08
Mer. Pass. 22 37.9		v −0.4 d 1.2		v 0.8 d 0.6		v 2.0 d 0.2		v 2.5 d 0.0		Saturn	33 16.8	20 25

Appendix H

1993 OCTOBER 10, 11, 12 (SUN., MON., TUES.)

UT (GMT)	SUN G.H.A.	SUN Dec.	MOON G.H.A.	v	Dec.	d	H.P.
10 00	183 13.2	S 6 33.8	255 58.7	9.3	N15 37.2	9.0	58.2
01	198 13.4	34.8	270 27.0	9.3	15 28.2	9.1	58.2
02	213 13.5	35.7	284 55.3	9.3	15 19.1	9.2	58.3
03	228 13.7	.. 36.7	299 23.6	9.3	15 09.9	9.2	58.3
04	243 13.9	37.6	313 51.9	9.4	15 00.7	9.4	58.4
05	258 14.0	38.6	328 20.3	9.3	14 51.3	9.5	58.4
06	273 14.2	S 6 39.5	342 48.6	9.3	N14 41.8	9.6	58.4
07	288 14.3	40.5	357 16.9	9.4	14 32.2	9.7	58.5
08	303 14.5	41.4	11 45.3	9.3	14 22.5	9.7	58.5
S 09	318 14.7	.. 42.4	26 13.6	9.3	14 12.8	9.9	58.5
U 10	333 14.8	43.3	40 41.9	9.4	14 02.9	9.9	58.6
N 11	348 15.0	44.3	55 10.3	9.3	13 53.0	10.1	58.6
D 12	3 15.2	S 6 45.2	69 38.6	9.4	N13 42.9	10.1	58.7
A 13	18 15.3	46.2	84 07.0	9.3	13 32.8	10.3	58.7
Y 14	33 15.5	47.1	98 35.3	9.4	13 22.5	10.3	58.7
15	48 15.7	.. 48.0	113 03.7	9.3	13 12.2	10.4	58.8
16	63 15.8	49.0	127 32.0	9.4	13 01.8	10.5	58.8
17	78 16.0	49.9	142 00.4	9.4	12 51.3	10.6	58.9
18	93 16.1	S 6 50.9	156 28.8	9.3	N12 40.7	10.6	58.9
19	108 16.3	51.8	170 57.1	9.4	12 30.1	10.8	58.9
20	123 16.5	52.8	185 25.5	9.3	12 19.3	10.8	59.0
21	138 16.6	.. 53.7	199 53.8	9.4	12 08.5	11.0	59.0
22	153 16.8	54.7	214 22.2	9.4	11 57.5	11.0	59.0
23	168 17.0	55.6	228 50.6	9.3	11 46.5	11.1	59.1
11 00	183 17.1	S 6 56.5	243 18.9	9.4	N11 35.4	11.1	59.1
01	198 17.3	57.5	257 47.3	9.4	11 24.3	11.3	59.2
02	213 17.4	58.4	272 15.7	9.3	11 13.0	11.3	59.2
03	228 17.6	6 59.4	286 44.0	9.4	11 01.7	11.4	59.2
04	243 17.8	7 00.3	301 12.4	9.4	10 50.3	11.5	59.3
05	258 17.9	01.3	315 40.8	9.3	10 38.8	11.6	59.3
06	273 18.1	S 7 02.2	330 09.1	9.4	N10 27.2	11.6	59.3
07	288 18.2	03.2	344 37.5	9.3	10 15.6	11.7	59.4
08	303 18.4	04.1	359 05.8	9.4	10 03.9	11.8	59.4
M 09	318 18.6	05.0	13 34.2	9.3	9 52.1	11.9	59.4
O 10	333 18.7	06.0	28 02.5	9.4	9 40.2	11.9	59.5
N 11	348 18.9	06.9	42 30.9	9.3	9 28.3	12.0	59.5
D 12	3 19.0	S 7 07.9	56 59.2	9.4	N 9 16.3	12.1	59.6
A 13	18 19.2	08.8	71 27.6	9.3	9 04.2	12.1	59.6
Y 14	33 19.4	09.8	85 55.9	9.3	8 52.1	12.2	59.6
15	48 19.5	.. 10.7	100 24.2	9.3	8 39.9	12.3	59.7
16	63 19.7	11.6	114 52.5	9.4	8 27.6	12.3	59.7
17	78 19.8	12.6	129 20.9	9.3	8 15.3	12.4	59.7
18	93 20.0	S 7 13.5	143 49.2	9.3	N 8 02.9	12.5	59.8
19	108 20.1	14.5	158 17.5	9.2	7 50.4	12.5	59.8
20	123 20.3	15.4	172 45.7	9.3	7 37.9	12.6	59.8
21	138 20.5	.. 16.3	187 14.0	9.3	7 25.3	12.6	59.9
22	153 20.6	17.3	201 42.3	9.3	7 12.7	12.7	59.9
23	168 20.8	18.2	216 10.6	9.2	7 00.0	12.7	59.9
12 00	183 20.9	S 7 19.2	230 38.8	9.3	N 6 47.3	12.9	60.0
01	198 21.1	20.1	245 07.1	9.2	6 34.4	12.8	60.0
02	213 21.2	21.0	259 35.3	9.2	6 21.6	12.9	60.0
03	228 21.4	.. 21.9	274 03.5	9.2	6 08.7	13.0	60.1
04	243 21.6	22.9	288 31.7	9.2	5 55.7	13.0	60.1
05	258 21.7	23.9	302 59.9	9.2	5 42.7	13.1	60.1
06	273 21.9	S 7 24.8	317 28.1	9.2	N 5 29.6	13.1	60.2
07	288 22.0	25.7	331 56.3	9.1	5 16.5	13.1	60.2
T 08	303 22.2	26.7	346 24.4	9.2	5 03.4	13.2	60.2
U 09	318 22.3	.. 27.6	0 52.6	9.1	4 50.2	13.3	60.3
E 10	333 22.5	28.6	15 20.7	9.1	4 36.9	13.3	60.3
S 11	348 22.6	29.5	29 48.8	9.1	4 23.6	13.3	60.3
D 12	3 22.8	S 7 30.4	44 16.9	9.1	N 4 10.3	13.4	60.4
A 13	18 23.0	31.4	58 45.0	9.0	3 56.9	13.4	60.4
Y 14	33 23.1	32.3	73 13.0	9.0	3 43.5	13.4	60.4
15	48 23.3	.. 33.2	87 41.0	9.1	3 30.1	13.5	60.4
16	63 23.4	34.2	102 09.1	9.0	3 16.6	13.5	60.5
17	78 23.6	35.1	116 37.1	8.9	3 03.1	13.5	60.5
18	93 23.7	S 7 36.1	131 05.0	9.0	N 2 49.6	13.6	60.5
19	108 23.9	37.0	145 33.0	8.9	2 36.0	13.6	60.6
20	123 24.0	37.9	160 00.9	8.9	2 22.4	13.6	60.6
21	138 24.2	.. 38.8	174 28.8	8.9	2 08.8	13.7	60.6
22	153 24.3	39.8	188 56.7	8.9	1 55.1	13.7	60.6
23	168 24.5	40.7	203 24.6	8.8	1 41.4	13.7	60.7
	S.D. 16.0	d 0.9	S.D. 16.0		16.2		16.4

Moonrise

Lat.	Twilight Naut.	Civil	Sunrise	10	11	12	13
N 72	04 37	05 56	07 05	23 08	25 20	01 20	03 30
N 70	04 43	05 54	06 56	23 29	25 30	01 30	03 31
68	04 48	05 52	06 49	23 46	25 38	01 38	03 31
66	04 52	05 51	06 43	23 59	25 44	01 44	03 32
64	04 55	05 50	06 38	24 09	00 09	01 50	03 32
62	04 57	05 49	06 33	24 19	00 19	01 54	03 33
60	04 59	05 48	06 29	24 26	00 26	01 58	03 33
N 58	05 01	05 47	06 26	24 33	00 33	02 02	03 33
56	05 03	05 46	06 23	24 39	00 39	02 05	03 34
54	05 04	05 45	06 20	24 45	00 45	02 08	03 34
52	05 05	05 44	06 18	24 49	00 49	02 10	03 34
50	05 06	05 43	06 15	24 54	00 54	02 13	03 34
45	05 07	05 41	06 10	25 03	01 03	02 18	03 35
N 40	05 08	05 39	06 06	00 03	01 11	02 22	03 35
35	05 08	05 37	06 03	00 12	01 18	02 26	03 35
30	05 07	05 35	05 59	00 20	01 24	02 29	03 36
20	05 06	05 31	05 54	00 35	01 34	02 34	03 36
N 10	05 03	05 27	05 48	00 47	01 43	02 39	03 37
0	04 58	05 23	05 43	00 59	01 51	02 44	03 37
S 10	04 53	05 17	05 38	01 10	02 00	02 48	03 37
20	04 45	05 11	05 33	01 23	02 08	02 53	03 38
30	04 34	05 02	05 27	01 37	02 18	02 59	03 39
35	04 27	04 57	05 23	01 45	02 24	03 02	03 39
40	04 18	04 51	05 19	01 54	02 31	03 05	03 39
45	04 08	04 44	05 14	02 05	02 38	03 10	03 40
S 50	03 54	04 34	05 08	02 18	02 48	03 15	03 40
52	03 47	04 30	05 05	02 24	02 52	03 17	03 41
54	03 40	04 25	05 02	02 31	02 56	03 19	03 41
56	03 32	04 20	04 59	02 38	03 01	03 22	03 41
58	03 22	04 14	04 55	02 46	03 07	03 25	03 42
S 60	03 10	04 07	04 51	02 56	03 13	03 28	03 42

Moonset

Lat.	Sunset	Twilight Civil	Naut.	10	11	12	13
N 72	16 27	17 35	18 53	16 28	16 07	15 50	15 34
N 70	16 36	17 38	18 48	16 05	15 55	15 46	15 37
68	16 43	17 39	18 43	15 48	15 45	15 42	15 39
66	16 49	17 41	18 40	15 33	15 37	15 39	15 41
64	16 54	17 42	18 37	15 21	15 30	15 37	15 43
62	16 59	17 43	18 35	15 11	15 24	15 35	15 45
60	17 03	17 45	18 33	15 02	15 18	15 33	15 46
N 58	17 06	17 46	18 31	14 55	15 14	15 31	15 47
56	17 10	17 47	18 30	14 48	15 10	15 29	15 48
54	17 12	17 48	18 29	14 42	15 06	15 28	15 49
52	17 15	17 49	18 28	14 36	15 02	15 27	15 50
50	17 17	17 50	18 27	14 31	14 59	15 25	15 51
45	17 22	17 52	18 26	14 20	14 52	15 23	15 53
N 40	17 27	17 54	18 25	14 11	14 47	15 21	15 55
35	17 30	17 56	18 25	14 03	14 42	15 19	15 56
30	17 34	17 58	18 26	13 56	14 37	15 17	15 57
20	17 40	18 02	18 27	13 44	14 30	15 14	15 59
N 10	17 45	18 06	18 31	13 34	14 23	15 11	16 01
0	17 50	18 11	18 35	13 24	14 16	15 09	16 02
S 10	17 55	18 16	18 41	13 14	14 10	15 06	16 04
20	18 01	18 23	18 49	13 03	14 03	15 04	16 06
30	18 07	18 32	19 00	12 50	13 55	15 00	16 08
35	18 11	18 37	19 07	12 43	13 50	14 59	16 09
40	18 16	18 43	19 16	12 35	13 45	14 56	16 10
45	18 21	18 51	19 27	12 25	13 38	14 54	16 12
S 50	18 27	19 00	19 41	12 13	13 31	14 51	16 13
52	18 30	19 05	19 48	12 08	13 27	14 50	16 14
54	18 33	19 10	19 55	12 02	13 24	14 48	16 15
56	18 36	19 15	20 04	11 55	13 19	14 46	16 16
58	18 40	19 22	20 14	11 48	13 15	14 45	16 17
S 60	18 44	19 29	20 26	11 39	13 09	14 43	16 18

Day	SUN Eqn. of Time 00h	12h	Mer. Pass.	MOON Mer. Pass. Upper	Lower	Age	Phase
10	12 52	13 00	11 47	07 11	19 38	24	◐
11	13 08	13 16	11 47	08 04	20 30	25	
12	13 23	13 31	11 46	08 56	21 23	26	

Appendix I

T 33°N

Hc	Zn	Hc	Zn	Hc	Zn	Hc	Zn	Hc	Zn	Hc	Zn	Hc	Zn
◆VEGA		Alphecca		ARCTURUS		◆SPICA		REGULUS		◆POLLUX		Dubhe	
13 41	052	43 34	083	56 49	106	41 26	152	56 54	237	35 42	283	59 49	347
14 21	053	44 24	083	57 37	107	41 50	153	56 11	238	34 53	283	59 37	346
15 02	053	45 14	084	58 25	108	42 12	154	55 28	240	34 04	284	59 25	345
15 42	054	46 04	084	59 13	109	42 34	155	54 44	241	33 15	284	59 11	344
16 23	054	46 54	085	60 00	110	42 54	157	54 00	242	32 26	285	58 57	343
17 03	054	47 45	085	60 47	111	43 14	158	53 16	243	31 37	285	58 43	343
17 44	055	48 35	086	61 34	112	43 32	159	52 31	244	30 49	285	58 27	342
18 26	055	49 25	086	62 21	113	43 49	160	51 45	245	30 00	286	58 11	341
19 07	056	50 15	087	63 07	114	44 06	162	51 00	246	29 12	286	57 55	340
19 49	056	51 05	087	63 52	116	44 21	163	50 14	247	28 24	287	57 38	340
20 30	056	51 56	088	64 37	117	44 35	164	49 27	248	27 36	287	57 20	339
21 12	057	52 46	088	65 22	118	44 48	166	48 40	249	26 48	287	57 02	338
21 55	057	53 36	089	66 06	120	45 00	167	47 53	250	26 00	288	56 43	338
22 37	057	54 27	089	66 49	121	45 10	169	47 06	250	25 12	288	56 23	337
23 19	058	55 17	090	67 32	123	45 20	170	46 18	251	24 24	289	56 03	336
◆Kochab		VEGA		Rasalhague		◆ANTARES		SPICA		◆REGULUS		Dubhe	
46 36	011	24 02	058	24 36	091	12 33	133	45 28	171	45 31	252	55 43	336
46 45	010	24 45	058	25 26	091	13 09	134	45 35	173	44 43	253	55 22	335
46 54	010	25 28	059	26 16	092	13 45	135	45 41	174	43 55	254	55 01	335
47 02	010	26 11	059	27 06	092	14 20	136	45 45	175	43 06	254	54 39	334
47 11	009	26 54	059	27 57	093	14 55	136	45 49	177	42 18	255	54 17	334
47 18	009	27 38	060	28 47	093	15 30	137	45 51	178	41 29	256	53 55	333
47 26	009	28 21	060	29 37	094	16 04	138	45 52	180	40 40	257	53 32	333
47 33	008	29 05	060	30 27	095	16 38	138	45 52	181	39 51	257	53 09	332
47 40	008	29 49	061	31 17	095	17 11	139	45 50	182	39 02	258	52 45	332
47 47	007	30 33	061	32 08	096	17 44	140	45 47	184	38 13	259	52 21	331
47 54	007	31 17	061	32 58	096	18 16	141	45 43	185	37 23	259	51 57	331
48 00	007	32 01	062	33 48	097	18 47	141	45 38	187	36 34	260	51 33	331
48 05	006	32 45	062	34 37	098	19 19	142	45 31	188	35 44	261	51 08	330
48 11	006	33 30	062	35 27	098	19 49	143	45 24	189	34 54	261	50 43	330
48 16	006	34 14	063	36 17	099	20 19	144	45 15	191	34 05	262	50 17	330
◆Kochab		VEGA		Rasalhague		◆ANTARES		SPICA		◆REGULUS		Dubhe	
48 20	005	34 59	063	37 07	100	20 49	145	45 05	192	33 15	263	49 52	329
48 25	005	35 44	063	37 56	100	21 18	145	44 53	194	32 25	263	49 26	329
48 29	004	36 29	063	38 46	101	21 46	146	44 41	195	31 35	264	49 00	329
48 32	004	37 14	064	39 35	102	22 14	147	44 28	196	30 45	264	48 34	328
48 36	004	37 59	064	40 24	102	22 41	148	44 13	198	29 55	265	48 07	328
48 39	003	38 44	064	41 13	103	23 07	149	43 57	199	29 04	266	47 40	328
48 41	003	39 30	064	42 02	104	23 33	150	43 40	200	28 14	266	47 14	328
48 44	002	40 15	065	42 51	104	23 58	150	43 22	202	27 24	267	46 47	327
48 45	002	41 00	065	43 40	105	24 23	151	43 03	203	26 34	267	46 20	327
48 47	002	41 46	065	44 28	106	24 47	152	42 43	204	25 44	268	45 52	327
48 48	001	42 32	065	45 17	107	25 10	153	42 22	205	24 53	268	45 25	327
48 49	001	43 18	066	46 05	107	25 32	154	42 00	207	24 03	269	44 57	327
48 49	000	44 03	066	46 53	108	25 54	155	41 37	208	23 13	269	44 30	327
48 49	000	44 49	066	47 40	109	26 15	156	41 14	209	22 22	270	44 02	326
48 49	359	45 35	066	48 28	110	26 35	157	40 49	210	21 32	271	43 34	326
DENEB		VEGA		◆ALTAIR		ANTARES		◆SPICA		Denebola		◆Dubhe	
25 47	051	46 21	066	19 20	092	26 55	158	40 23	211	43 02	259	43 06	326
26 27	051	47 07	067	20 11	092	27 14	159	39 56	212	42 13	259	42 38	326
27 06	052	47 54	067	21 01	093	27 32	160	39 29	214	41 23	260	42 10	326
27 46	052	48 40	067	21 51	094	27 49	160	39 01	215	40 34	261	41 42	326
28 26	052	49 26	067	22 41	094	28 05	161	38 32	216	39 44	261	41 14	326
29 05	053	50 13	067	23 32	095	28 21	162	38 02	217	38 54	262	40 45	326
29 45	053	50 59	067	24 22	095	28 36	163	37 32	218	38 04	263	40 17	326
30 26	053	51 45	068	25 12	096	28 50	164	37 00	219	37 14	263	39 49	326
31 06	053	52 32	068	26 02	096	29 03	165	36 28	220	36 24	264	39 20	326
31 46	054	53 19	068	26 52	097	29 15	166	35 56	221	35 34	265	38 52	326
32 27	054	54 05	068	27 42	098	29 27	167	35 22	222	34 44	265	38 24	326
33 07	054	54 52	068	28 31	098	29 37	168	34 48	223	33 54	266	37 55	326
33 48	054	55 38	068	29 21	099	29 47	169	34 14	224	33 04	266	37 27	326
34 29	054	56 25	068	30 11	100	29 56	170	33 39	225	32 13	267	36 59	326
35 10	055	57 12	068	31 00	100	30 04	171	33 03	226	31 23	267	36 30	326
◆DENEB		ALTAIR		Nunki		◆ANTARES		SPICA		ARCTURUS		◆Alkaid	
35 51	055	31 50	101	17 34	139	30 11	172	32 26	227	62 54	246	60 32	314
36 32	055	32 39	101	18 07	140	30 17	173	31 49	228	62 07	247	59 55	313
37 14	055	33 29	102	18 39	141	30 22	175	31 12	229	61 21	248	59 18	313
37 55	055	34 18	103	19 10	142	30 26	176	30 34	229	60 34	249	58 41	312
38 37	056	35 07	103	19 41	143	30 30	177	29 56	230	59 47	250	58 04	312
39 18	056	35 56	104	20 11	143	30 32	178	29 17	231	58 59	251	57 26	312
40 00	056	36 44	105	20 41	144	30 34	179	28 37	232	58 11	252	56 49	311
40 41	056	37 33	106	21 10	145	30 35	180	27 58	233	57 23	253	56 11	311
41 23	056	38 21	106	21 39	146	30 34	181	27 17	234	56 35	254	55 33	311
42 05	056	39 10	107	22 07	147	30 33	182	26 37	234	55 46	255	54 54	310
42 47	056	39 58	108	22 34	147	30 31	183	25 55	235	54 58	256	54 16	310
43 29	057	40 45	109	23 01	148	30 28	184	25 14	236	54 09	257	53 38	310
44 11	057	41 33	109	23 27	149	30 25	185	24 32	237	53 20	258	52 59	310
44 53	057	42 20	110	23 53	150	30 20	186	23 50	237	52 30	258	52 20	310
45 35	057	43 08	111	24 18	151	30 14	187	23 07	238	51 41	259	51 42	310
◆DENEB		ALTAIR		Nunki		◆ANTARES		ARCTURUS		◆Alkaid		Kochab	
46 17	057	43 54	112	24 42	152	30 08	188	50 52	260	51 03	309	45 50	348
46 59	057	44 41	113	25 06	153	30 00	189	50 02	261	50 24	309	45 39	348
47 42	057	45 27	113	25 28	153	29 52	190	49 12	261	49 45	309	45 28	347
48 24	057	46 13	114	25 51	154	29 43	191	48 23	262	49 06	309	45 17	347
49 06	057	46 59	115	26 12	155	29 32	192	47 33	263	48 27	309	45 06	347
49 48	057	47 44	116	26 33	156	29 22	193	46 43	263	47 48	309	44 54	347
50 30	057	48 29	117	26 53	157	29 10	194	45 53	264	47 09	309	44 42	346
51 13	057	49 14	118	27 12	158	28 57	195	45 03	265	46 30	309	44 30	346
51 55	057	49 58	119	27 30	159	28 44	196	44 13	265	45 51	309	44 18	346
52 37	057	50 42	120	27 48	160	28 29	197	43 22	266	45 11	309	44 05	345
53 19	057	51 25	121	28 05	161	28 14	198	42 32	266	44 32	309	43 53	345
54 01	057	52 08	122	28 21	162	27 58	199	41 42	267	43 53	309	43 40	345
54 43	057	52 50	124	28 36	163	27 41	200	40 52	268	43 14	309	43 26	345
55 25	057	53 32	125	28 50	164	27 24	201	40 01	268	42 35	309	43 13	345
56 07	056	54 13	126	29 04	165	27 05	202	39 11	269	41 56	309	43 00	344

LAT 33°N

LHA ♈	Hc	Zn	Hc	Zn	Hc	Zn	Hc	Zn	Hc	Zn	Hc	Zn	Hc	Zn
	◆DENEB		ALTAIR		◆Nunki		ANTARES		ARCTURUS		◆Alkaid		Kochab	
270	56 49	056	54 53	127	29 16	166	26 46	203	38 21	269	41 17	309	42 46	344
271	57 31	056	55 33	128	29 28	167	26 26	204	37 31	270	40 38	309	42 32	344
272	58 13	056	56 12	130	29 39	168	26 06	205	36 40	270	40 00	309	42 18	344
273	58 55	056	56 50	131	29 49	169	25 44	206	35 50	271	39 21	310	42 04	344
274	59 36	055	57 28	133	29 59	170	25 22	206	35 00	271	38 42	310	41 50	343
275	60 17	055	58 04	134	30 07	171	25 00	207	34 09	272	38 03	310	41 35	343
276	60 59	055	58 40	136	30 14	172	24 36	208	33 19	272	37 25	310	41 21	343
277	61 40	055	59 15	137	30 21	173	24 12	209	32 29	273	36 46	310	41 06	343
278	62 21	054	59 48	139	30 27	174	23 47	210	31 39	273	36 08	310	40 51	343
279	63 01	054	60 21	140	30 32	175	23 22	211	30 48	274	35 29	310	40 36	343
280	63 42	053	60 53	142	30 35	176	22 55	212	29 58	274	34 51	311	40 21	342
281	64 22	053	61 23	144	30 38	177	22 29	213	29 08	275	34 13	311	40 06	342
282	65 02	052	61 52	146	30 40	178	22 01	213	28 18	276	33 35	311	39 51	342
283	65 42	052	62 20	147	30 42	179	21 33	214	27 28	276	32 57	311	39 35	342
284	66 21	051	62 46	149	30 42	180	21 05	215	26 38	277	32 19	311	39 20	342
	◆Alpheratz		Enif		ALTAIR		◆ANTARES		ARCTURUS		◆Alkaid		Kochab	
285	25 25	071	45 48	112	63 11	151	20 36	216	25 48	277	31 41	311	39 04	342
286	26 12	071	46 35	113	63 34	153	20 06	217	24 58	277	31 03	312	38 48	342
287	27 00	071	47 21	114	63 56	155	19 36	217	24 08	278	30 26	312	38 33	342
288	27 47	072	48 07	115	64 16	158	19 05	218	23 18	278	29 48	312	38 17	342
289	28 35	072	48 52	116	64 34	160	18 33	219	22 28	279	29 11	312	38 01	342
290	29 23	073	49 37	117	64 51	162	18 01	220	21 39	279	28 34	313	37 45	341
291	30 11	073	50 22	118	65 05	164	17 29	220	20 49	280	27 57	313	37 29	341
292	30 59	073	51 07	119	65 18	167	16 56	221	20 00	280	27 20	313	37 13	341
293	31 48	074	51 50	120	65 29	169	16 23	222	19 10	281	26 43	313	36 57	341
294	32 36	074	52 34	121	65 37	171	15 49	223	18 21	281	26 07	314	36 40	341
295	33 25	075	53 17	122	65 44	174	15 14	223	17 32	282	25 31	314	36 24	341
296	34 13	075	53 59	123	65 48	176	14 40	224	16 42	282	24 54	314	36 08	341
297	35 02	075	54 41	124	65 51	178	14 04	225	15 53	283	24 18	314	35 52	341
298	35 51	076	55 22	126	65 51	181	13 29	225	15 04	283	23 42	315	35 35	341
299	36 39	076	56 03	127	65 49	183	12 53	226	14 15	284	23 07	315	35 19	341
	◆Mirfak		Alpheratz		◆FOMALHAUT		ALTAIR		Rasalhague		◆Alphecca		Kochab	
300	12 51	038	37 28	077	14 35	141	65 45	186	51 05	247	33 02	283	35 03	341
301	13 23	039	38 17	077	15 06	142	65 39	188	50 18	248	32 13	283	34 46	341
302	13 54	039	39 06	077	15 37	143	65 31	190	49 31	249	31 24	283	34 30	341
303	14 26	039	39 55	078	16 08	143	65 21	193	48 44	250	30 35	284	34 14	341
304	14 58	040	40 45	078	16 37	144	65 09	195	47 57	251	29 46	284	33 57	341
305	15 30	040	41 34	079	17 07	145	64 55	197	47 09	251	28 57	285	33 41	341
306	16 03	040	42 23	079	17 35	146	64 39	200	46 22	252	28 09	285	33 24	341
307	16 35	041	43 13	079	18 04	146	64 21	202	45 34	253	27 20	286	33 08	341
308	17 08	041	44 02	080	18 31	147	64 02	204	44 45	254	26 32	286	32 52	341
309	17 42	041	44 52	080	18 58	148	63 40	206	43 57	255	25 43	286	32 36	341
310	18 15	042	45 41	081	19 25	149	63 17	208	43 08	255	24 55	287	32 19	341
311	18 49	042	46 31	081	19 51	149	62 53	210	42 20	256	24 07	287	32 03	341
312	19 22	042	47 21	081	20 16	150	62 27	212	41 31	257	23 19	288	31 47	341
313	19 57	043	48 11	082	20 41	151	62 00	214	40 42	258	22 31	288	31 31	341
314	20 31	043	49 00	082	21 05	152	61 31	216	39 52	258	21 43	289	31 15	341
	◆Mirfak		Hamal		Diphda		◆FOMALHAUT		ALTAIR		◆VEGA		Kochab	
315	21 05	043	23 10	076	16 14	125	21 28	153	61 01	217	60 37	292	30 59	341
316	21 40	044	23 59	077	16 55	126	21 51	154	60 30	219	59 50	292	30 43	342
317	22 15	044	24 48	077	17 35	126	22 13	154	59 57	221	59 03	292	30 27	342
318	22 50	044	25 37	078	18 16	127	22 34	155	59 24	222	58 17	292	30 11	342
319	23 25	045	26 26	078	18 56	128	22 55	156	58 49	224	57 30	292	29 55	342
320	24 01	045	27 15	079	19 35	128	23 15	157	58 14	226	56 43	292	29 40	342
321	24 36	045	28 05	079	20 15	129	23 34	158	57 37	227	55 56	292	29 24	342
322	25 12	045	28 54	079	20 53	130	23 52	159	57 00	228	55 10	292	29 08	342
323	25 48	046	29 44	080	21 32	131	24 10	160	56 22	230	54 23	292	28 53	342
324	26 24	046	30 33	080	22 10	132	24 27	161	55 43	231	53 36	292	28 38	342
325	27 00	046	31 23	081	22 47	132	24 44	162	55 04	232	52 50	292	28 22	342
326	27 37	046	32 13	081	23 24	133	24 59	162	54 24	234	52 03	292	28 07	342
327	28 13	047	33 02	082	24 01	134	25 14	163	53 43	235	51 17	293	27 52	343
328	28 50	047	33 52	082	24 37	135	25 28	164	53 01	236	50 30	293	27 37	343
329	29 27	047	34 42	083	25 12	135	25 41	165	52 19	237	49 44	293	27 22	343
	◆Mirfak		Hamal		Diphda		◆FOMALHAUT		ALTAIR		◆VEGA		Kochab	
330	30 04	047	35 32	083	25 47	136	25 54	166	51 36	238	48 58	293	27 07	343
331	30 41	048	36 22	084	26 22	137	26 05	167	50 53	239	48 11	293	26 53	343
332	31 18	048	37 12	084	26 56	138	26 16	168	50 10	241	47 25	293	26 38	343
333	31 55	048	38 02	085	27 29	139	26 26	169	49 26	242	46 39	294	26 24	343
334	32 33	048	38 52	085	28 02	140	26 35	170	48 41	243	45 53	294	26 09	344
335	33 10	048	39 42	086	28 34	141	26 44	171	47 56	244	45 07	294	25 55	344
336	33 48	049	40 33	086	29 06	142	26 51	172	47 11	244	44 21	294	25 41	344
337	34 26	049	41 23	087	29 36	142	26 58	173	46 26	245	43 35	294	25 27	344
338	35 04	049	42 13	087	30 07	143	27 04	174	45 40	246	42 49	295	25 14	344
339	35 42	049	43 03	088	30 36	144	27 09	175	44 54	247	42 04	295	25 00	344
340	36 20	049	43 54	088	31 05	145	27 13	176	44 07	248	41 18	295	24 46	345
341	36 58	049	44 44	089	31 34	146	27 16	177	43 20	249	40 32	295	24 33	345
342	37 36	049	45 34	089	32 01	147	27 19	178	42 33	250	39 47	296	24 20	345
343	38 14	050	46 24	090	32 28	148	27 20	179	41 46	250	39 02	296	24 07	345
344	38 53	050	47 15	090	32 54	149	27 21	180	40 58	251	38 16	296	23 54	345
	◆CAPELLA		ALDEBARAN		Diphda		◆FOMALHAUT		ALTAIR		◆VEGA		Kochab	
345	20 30	048	13 53	079	33 20	150	27 21	181	40 10	252	37 31	296	23 41	345
346	21 08	048	14 43	080	33 44	151	27 20	182	39 23	253	36 46	297	23 29	346
347	21 45	048	15 32	080	34 08	152	27 18	183	38 34	254	36 01	297	23 16	346
348	22 23	049	16 22	081	34 31	153	27 15	184	37 46	254	35 16	297	23 04	346
349	23 01	049	17 12	081	34 53	154	27 12	185	36 57	255	34 32	297	22 52	346
350	23 39	049	18 01	082	35 14	156	27 07	186	36 09	256	33 47	298	22 40	346
351	24 17	050	18 51	082	35 35	157	27 02	186	35 20	256	33 02	298	22 28	347
352	24 55	050	19 41	083	35 54	158	26 56	187	34 31	257	32 18	298	22 17	347
353	25 34	050	20 31	083	36 13	159	26 49	188	33 42	258	31 34	299	22 05	347
354	26 13	050	21 21	084	36 31	160	26 41	189	32 53	258	30 50	299	21 54	347
355	26 52	051	22 11	084	36 47	161	26 33	190	32 03	259	30 06	299	21 43	347
356	27 31	051	23 01	085	37 03	162	26 23	191	31 14	260	29 22	299	21 32	348
357	28 10	051	23 51	085	37 18	163	26 13	192	30 24	260	28 38	300	21 22	348
358	28 49	052	24 41	086	37 32	165	26 02	193	29 35	261	27 54	300	21 11	348
359	29 29	052	25 32	086	37 45	166	25 50	194	28 45	262	27 11	300	21 01	348

Index

Index